THE STRENGTHS OF A CHRISTIAN

SPIRITUALITY AND THE CHRISTIAN LIFE
Richard H. Bell, *Editor*

THE STRENGTHS OF A CHRISTIAN

ROBERT C. ROBERTS

WIPF & STOCK · Eugene, Oregon

Scripture quotations from the Revised Standard Version of the Bible are copyrighted 1946, 1952, © 1971, 1973 by the Division of Christian Education of the National Council of the Churches of Christ in the U.S.A., and are used by permission.

Chapter 1 originally appeared in somewhat different form as my article "What Is Spirituality?" in *The Reformed Journal*, August 1983.

Wipf and Stock Publishers
199 W 8th Ave, Suite 3
Eugene, OR 97401

The Strengths of a Christian
By Roberts, Robert C. and Bell, Richard H.
Copyright©1984 by Roberts, Robert C.
ISBN 13: 978-1-62564-024-6
Publication date 4/30/2013
Previously published by Westminster Press, 1984

*To my wife,
in whom
the strengths of a Christian
are so evident*

I remember my father said to me after a holiday, "I worried about you" and I said, "Did you think I'd had an accident?" He said, "That would have meant nothing, even if you had been killed. I thought you had lost your integrity."

Anthony Bloom
Beginning to Pray

CONTENTS

Editor's Introduction 11
Preface 15

Chapter One   Spirituality 17
Chapter Two   Self-control 30
Chapter Three Patience 53
Chapter Four Perseverance 83

List of Works Cited 117

EDITOR'S INTRODUCTION

In 1609 Francis de Sales published a helpful book designed "to instruct those who live in town, within families, or at court, and by their state of life are obliged to live an ordinary life." It was, as he said, "a collection of bits of good advice stated in plain, intelligible words." The book, *Introduction to the Devout Life*, became a "spiritual classic." Although we will not claim that the books in this series will become spiritual classics, they are intended for a similar reader—one "obliged to live an ordinary life," and they are written in "plain, intelligible words."

In terms of their subject matter, they share another point with Francis de Sales's book. He said about the Christian life that "a strong, resolute soul can live in the world without being infected by any of its moods." This was not an easy task then, nor is it now. But one of the goals of the Christian life is to free ourselves from circumstances that hinder love and service to God. When the apostle Paul spoke of having the "mind of Christ," he was asking that we not yield to the accidental features of this world; that we strive to free ourselves from being defined by the social, political, and economic contingencies of this world. A great effort of the spirit is needed to do this.

This series is intended to help its readers in this effort

of the spirit. We call these books spiritual because they deal with how God's Spirit intersects with the human spirit. They focus attention on the Bible as the principal source for hearing and understanding God's Spirit, and on the *self* as the agent for living in the spirit.

Again, Francis de Sales suggests a strategy that augurs well for the volumes in this series. He asks: "How can we fight against [our imperfections] unless we see them, or overcome them unless we face them?" And he answers: "Our victory does not consist in being unconscious of them but in not consenting to them, and not to consent to them is to be displeased with them." Growth in the spirit involves seeing and facing our imperfections, not consenting to them; it involves being displeased with them and having courage to suffer the wounds meted out by our world. Such growth is given its Christian shape by our memories and stories, by our inner life in its emptiness and fullness, its weakness and strength, as we relate to God as Emmanuel—"God with us." In this concept of *God with us* the series finds its foundation in what is traditionally called *spirituality*.

But more important in this series is how we come to discern God with us and activate our will to make sense of our lives. Thus a second focus is that of building character and its natural outflow in the life of a Christian. The Christian life comes down to how each person faithfully lives in the human community and makes that great effort of spirit in devotion to God and in daily moral and political service.

If no other books you have read lately have encouraged you to take hold of your self and your Christian life with courage and firmness, these books will. They will take you patiently through many identifiable thickets of human life and ask you when it was that you allowed God to speak to you, embrace you, and lead you. These books are intended to be traveling companions, guides to take you closer to the center of the Christian life, closer to the Bible, closer to yourself, and thus, it is hoped, closer to God.

In this book, *The Strengths of a Christian*, Bob Roberts places an important aspect of spirituality within our grasp. We are prodded to ask: "Have I really worked at being Christian? Do I understand myself and what I do each day in the light of the presence of God?"

In the "strength virtues," self-control, patience, and perseverance, Roberts says we have the tools to fight "inward dullness" and "outward pressures to give up our faith." And not only is this fight with our faith but also with dullness and pressures that get into and beset our ordinary lives: our work, our family life, our friendships. Roberts is especially colorful in his illustrations of "moments of adversity in the life of married love" and in dealing with our children when patience proves nearly impossible.

One of the remarkable things about this book is its style. In it you will find yourself, as I did so often. You will see yourself in your relationship to your next-door neighbor, your children, your spouse, and your boss, as well as in relationship to your own thoughts. So be prepared for a blush while reading, a twinge of guilt, a good laugh—and for help just when you recognize you need it most. This book offers hope to readers who sometimes think the press of it all is too great, or that the odds against inching or clawing your way to a measured and peaceful life are too overwhelming.

There is another side to this book, though. As we discover ourselves in his illustrations, we are also forced to think about why we are as we are. Roberts examines ordinary human motivations for our vices: our gluttony and pride, our imprudence and envy, our anger and unfaithfulness. So there is this balance between tough reasoned reflection that calls for tenacious reading, on the one hand, and memorable examples that remind us of our ordinary blunders and simple achievements, on the other hand.

Roberts says there is some "old-fashioned stuff about loving one another" in this book. But you will quickly discover that Roberts' "old-fashioned stuff" is fresh and encouraging to those who are weary in the struggle for a sensible Christian life and who seek a kind of decency that does not fade in the shadows of daily trials. He challenges us finally, as he says, "to become your own master in obedience to God who is master of all, to become his partner in the task of becoming solid enough, single enough, centered enough to belong to the community of spirits that is the kingdom of God."

RICHARD H. BELL

PREFACE

The idea to write on the strengths of a Christian came to me during my reflections about the Christian emotions—such virtues and acts of glory as rejoicing, hoping, giving thanks from the heart, and possessing the peace that passes understanding. For as I worked on the emotions, both reflectively and personally, it occurred to me that there is indeed such a thing as *working* on one's emotions. We have capacities to work on them. These capacities, when developed to some degree, constitute strength of character. The lists of Christian virtues that we find in the New Testament (sometimes called the "fruit" of the Holy Spirit) are not exhausted by these emotion words. Such traits as self-control, patience, perseverance, and courage are clearly not emotions but, to a large extent, capacities for working on emotions, for opposing the bad ones and encouraging the good ones. There is worth to exploring these capacities, to see what can be learned that might aid Christians in acquiring them.

I thank Don Campbell and Annie Ackerman of the Presbytery of South Louisiana for an invitation to lead a ministers' retreat in January of 1983, for which an early version of the material on patience was prepared. Alas, the retreat had to be canceled, but not before its prospect had squeezed these thoughts to the surface of my mind.

Thanks are also due to the National Endowment for the Humanities for a wonderful summer seminar directed by Jim Dittes of Yale University in June–August of 1983. The seminar, Freedom and Religious Personality, fit with the present book, since the Christian traits of self-control, patience, and perseverance presuppose, and are the development of, freedom in one or more senses of that ambiguous word. During the period of the seminar I worked on perseverance, and I thank Jim Dittes for his critical comments and generous encouragement.

My friends Richard Bell, Dennis Okholm, Richard Olmsted, and Elizabeth Vanderkooy Roberts all read the manuscript at one stage or another and improved it greatly with their suggestions. To Elizabeth, who is not only a friend but also my wife, I dedicate this book. And finally I must thank my dear children Nathan and Beth for all that they have taught me about self-control and patience.

R.C.R.

CHAPTER ONE
SPIRITUALITY

From the looks of shelves in campus bookstores and other seemingly respectable places, there is a hunger abroad in the land. The word "spirituality" is in the air in such unlikely habitats as Protestant seminaries and even your odd Presbyterian church. What does it all mean? Is it the fading maturation of the charismatic movement? A rebellion against politics? Superstition? The surreptitious return of the true church? Me-generation navel gazing? Occultism turned (slightly) respectable? A learned historian friend of mine, a watcher of religious movements, overheard me once breathing that word at a social gathering. Later, when we were alone, he said to me a little skeptically, "Bob, someday you'll have to tell me what spirituality is." I intend to leave the question "What does it all mean?" to my historian friend, but *his* question is one I would like to have a go at.

Spiritualities

The word "spirit" richly evokes many things, but I suppose any account of human spirituality would point out that we, in contrast to our fellows in the animal world, live by adopted *conceptions* of what our life is and ought to be.

We impose order on ourselves and on our world by the way we "picture" things. And pictures abound. There is ethical humanist spirituality, health-freak spirituality, existentialist spirituality, stoic spirituality; there are various therapeutic spiritualities; there is consumerist spirituality, economic opportunity spirituality, moral majority spirituality—and, of course, Christian spirituality. Each of these pictures has its variants and in concrete instances, varying admixtures of other spiritualities. Each is a different conception of what human life is and ought to be, and each is controlled and shaped by a different set of leading concepts. Each involves, for the person who has imbibed a particular spirituality, a differing set of emotional responses, of judgments about what is appropriate, and of characteristic virtues and vices. An economic opportunist is a different kind of *person* from a Christian or an existentialist. Different pictures of life yield, if they are consistently applied, different *souls*.

For this reason it ought to be distressing to Christians when attempts are made to mix the Christian picture of self and world with the pictures that govern other spiritualities. For example, some types of business enterprises try to mix consumerist and economic opportunist spiritualities with the Christian one. The danger is that under pressure from the business worldview Christian concepts may be profoundly changed. A person may talk the Christian language and think himself or herself a Christian, while coming out on Judgment Day with a consumerist soul instead of a Christian one. The same danger exists when Christian theology is reinterpreted in terms of other spiritualities, such as the existentialist, Marxist, or psychotherapeutic ones. I am not saying that Christians have nothing to learn from existentialists, Marxists, and psychotherapists. But a difference exists between, say, gaining a Christian insight while reading Albert Ellis and importing elements of the Ellis spirituality in the name of the Christian one. It takes more conceptual finesse than most laypeople (and many theologians) have to distinguish between these. Paul makes it clear that he does not believe the Holy Spirit is the only spirit around. The Holy Spirit is in *competition* with other spirits, and for this reason, as Paul notes in his First Letter to the Corinthians (12:10), the Spirit's gifts to the church include "the ability to distinguish between spirits." Earlier in the same letter Paul, speaking of the church, says, "We have received not the spirit of the world, but the Spirit which is from God" (2:12).

"Being in the Spirit of . . . "

These remarks suggest that possessing (or being possessed by) the Holy Spirit is not only very *different* from possessing the spirit (or spirits) of the world but is also in some respects *similar* to possessing other spirits. In English we have a secular expression: "Being in the spirit of. . . . " By reflecting on this expression and a couple of things that people can be in the spirit of, we may get some insight into what spirituality—in particular, Christian spirituality—is.

Let me start with a superficial but, I think, informative example. To be in the spirit of Christmas is to be in the grip of a jolly benevolence, a kind of generosity and friendliness and self-abandon to which most of us are not accustomed for much of the year. There is a kind of infectiousness to the spirit of Christmas. No doubt you can do some things to foster it, but if you succeed, having this spirit is not something you *do* but something that *happens* to you. When in the midst of people among whom the spirit of Christmas is really moving, you often catch that spirit without trying—maybe even when you are trying not to. And you catch it not only from other people but also from cues: pine needles, Christmas carols, or certain puddings.

The spirit of some churches is like that of Christmas. The holiness envelops you like an atmosphere, comes down on you and grabs you almost without your consent. Again, it is not just the other people who have infected you; there are those cues: the language of faith, the hymns, the windows and shades of light and darkness in the sanctuary, the smells. You are caught up in the spirit of the thing; maybe it's even the Spirit.

Another instance of "being in the spirit of . . . " is the relation of some Stoic philosophers to Socrates. They lived in a kind of imaginal communion with him, trying to mirror his character in their own. By reflecting on written accounts of Socrates they sought to emulate his lighthearted indifference to money, reputation, and personal safety and his enthusiasm for personal integrity. Their object was not so much to imitate his actions—this would be an easier and less "spiritual" task—but to imitate his attitudes, his patterns of emotional response, his ways of thinking about himself and others. They sought to live in the spirit of Socrates. Epictetus follows up some advice on Stoic living with these words:

> This was how Socrates attained perfection, paying heed to nothing but reason, in all that he encountered. And if you are not yet Socrates, yet ought you to live as one who would wish to be a Socrates. (*Enchiridion* No. 51)

Being in the spirit of Socrates differs in three ways from being in the spirit of Christmas (apart from the obvious fact that these are different spirits). The spirit of Socrates belongs to a real person, even if the only way to commune with him (since he is dead) is through literature. But the spirit of Christmas is not *somebody's* spirit. Certainly it is not that of Santa Claus; more plausibly, Santa Claus gets his spirit from the spirit of Christmas. The spirit of Christmas is a social atmosphere that makes no reference to any personality. But these two spirits are similar in this way: The spirit of a person like Socrates can *generate* a social atmosphere. You can easily imagine, I think, how Socrates' influence might have been felt as an atmosphere in a meeting of a Stoic teacher with his pupils. And I do not doubt that when the spirit of Socrates was thus moving in their midst, there was something infectious about it, just like the spirit of Christmas.

But being in the spirit of Socrates, as a Stoic might have been, was something much deeper. The spirit of Christmas is unlike deeper spiritualities in that being in it is expected to be a passing thing. Being seasonal, it is a moodlike condition rather than a determination of *character*. No one accuses you of fickleness or superficiality if the spirit of Christmas leaves you when the carols stop sounding and the tinsel is taken down. But if the spirit of Socrates was only a mood that gripped you in meetings, your teacher would rightly judge that you had not yet really got the spirit of Socrates.

The third difference is related to the second. Because the spirit of Socrates is a monumental achievement and not a condition that one slips into through inattention, getting into the spirit of Socrates is likewise a strenuous affair, requiring self-discipline, long-term guidance, and the deliberate focusing of one's mind. At a party we may be gripped in spite of ourselves by the spirit of Christmas, but entering into the spirit of Socrates involves intentional hard work and a good deal of suffering.

Christian Spirituality

While Christian spirituality does, in a small respect, resemble the spirit of Christmas, it has much more in common with the Socratic spirituality of the Stoics. The Spirit of the Christian personality is a real person; the spirituality itself is the possession of deeply etched and stable character traits, some of which mirror the character of the primary Spirit; and these are learned by a long and arduous process of guided discipline.

The main formal difference between Christian spirituality and Socratic spirituality is that the character traits of the former are learned and exemplified through intercourse with the One whose fruits they are. I spoke of "communion" with Socrates, but here we are speaking of literal communion. In the normal course of the spiritual life, God is *present* to believers and in *conversation* and *interaction* with them. It is true that God's character is not known, except through Scripture, in sufficient detail for Christian spirituality; just as Socrates' character is known to a Stoic only through a written record. It is also true that God's presence, like the "presence" of Socrates, is mediated largely through the human mental powers of conceptualization and imagination. But it would be wrong to conclude from these facts that in prayer and meditation and daily conscious action God is present to the believer only in the sense in which Socrates is "present" to the Stoic.

Christian spirituality is a set of character traits that blossom when somebody appropriates the picture of self and world embodied in the story of God's actions toward humankind in Jesus of Nazareth. They are referred to in the New Testament as "fruit"—fruit of faith, of righteousness, of the gospel, of Jesus Christ as the Vine, and of the Holy Spirit. They are traits such as hope, joy, peace, gratitude, compassion, generosity, gentleness, kindness, confidence, self-control, patience, and perseverance. Such traits are what make a person a Christian; they are the "definition" of the Christian spirituality. As this list suggests, there is considerable psychological richness here: A Christian spirit is many-faceted and offers enormous potential for sensitive, edifying exploration. It also suggests the distortion that Christian spirituality is likely to suffer when a thinker alights on some single "essence" of spirituality such as simplicity or openness to the future or authenticity or social justice. Such concepts probably capture *something* about Christian spirituality, but it is unlikely that any such essence hunting will preserve the richness of the biblical concept. Thinkers are sometimes led into this essence hunting by focusing their thought on large biblical words such as "faith" and "righteousness" rather than on little ones like "patience" and "gentleness," "peace" and "gratitude." There are at least three kinds of fruit of the Holy Spirit. I shall call these the emotions, the styles, and the strengths.

The Emotions

The most central traits of Christian spirituality are emotion-dispositions such as hope, peace, joy, compassion, and gratitude. An emotion is always a way of viewing something where the "view" touches one or more of our concerns. For me to be angry at someone, for example, is to view the person as offending in some action or omission or attitude about which he or she has some choice, and where the offense touches some concern of mine. The concern may be for my reputation, safety, self-esteem, spiritual welfare, or pocketbook, or for that of a friend; or indeed it may even be for the reputation, safety, and so on of the person at whom I am angry. All that is needed is that I see the person as offending in something that touches some concern of mine.

Similarly, Christianity is a way of viewing oneself and one's world, where the view touches on some deep concerns. Hope is a matter of viewing the future of oneself and the world as an eternal order in which the Father of Jesus is appropriately loved and revered. Peace is viewing God as your provider and protector in whatever situations of destitution and violence and insecurity you find yourself, and seeing yourself as no longer an enemy of God but reconciled by the blood of Jesus. Compassion is seeing my suffering or deficient neighbor as a fellow child of the kingdom with whom Christ has identified as he has identified with me. But these ways of "viewing" are not emotions unless I care deeply about what I "see." I have to yearn for the kingdom, seek it, treasure it, desire it, before the vision it gives me will amount to Christian spirituality—that is, will amount to hope, peace, joy, compassion, and gratitude as genuine emotions. If I am content with my present worldly life, successfully denying the prospect of death and complacent about the evil in the world's heart and in my own, then the message of the kingdom will not bear these fruits in me even if in some sense I believe it.

If these fruits are emotions, and emotions are ways of "seeing" things, we can see how important meditation will be in developing the fruits of the Spirit. We will have to be *trained* in seeing, and this training, like Stoic training in the spirit of Socrates, is one which goes against the easy self-understandings of our environment and the natural inclinations of our hearts. But the Christian life is not just a meditative expectation of the kingdom. It is a life of communion with God. It is fellowship with God, prayer and listening, training by Jesus himself. Stoics are not trained by Socrates; instead, they train *themselves* with the help of some documents about Socrates. But Christians do not train themselves with the help of some documents about Jesus; Jesus lives, and with the help of the Christian documents he communes with his people. They pray to him, listen for his voice, encounter him in their needy neighbor.

And so the Christian life is more like living in God's home. It is like learning from an earthly parent who gives you a vision of how things are going to be and leads you in his or her way, rewarding your obedience and chastising your waywardness but through it all nurturing you and giving you peace. There is a spirit that moves in God's home; it is the Spirit of God. And getting possessed by this Spirit is what happens to those who dwell in the home of the Lord all the days of their life—who are nurtured by this environment of hope, compassion, and peace. Because Christian spirituality is a kind of intercourse, prayer and the church are its central foci: prayer as conversation with God, and the church as God's "home," the place where he especially dwells, his earthly presence, his "body."

The Styles

The image of Christians as children dwelling in the home of their Parent and Elder Brother evokes the strand of spirituality called "the imitation of Christ" and calls to mind the passages in Scripture where Christians are called on to imitate God. Most of the character traits I mentioned in the last section are *not* imitations of God. God does not hope for the kingdom but simply appoints it. God is not grateful to himself, at least not in anything like the way his human creatures are expected to be grateful to him. God is not at peace with himself as his children are, because he has never distrusted himself or been at enmity with himself. But God does have a number of character traits that the Christian is expected to mirror. These reflections too are fruits of God's Spirit; I shall call them "styles." I am thinking of such spiritual traits as gentleness, nurturing of the poor and abandoned, forgiveness, mercy, long-suffering, and kindness to enemies. These are not emotions; they are attitudes and patterns of behavioral response. (One excepton that comes to mind is compassion, which is both an emotion and a style.)

Of course it is possible for non-Christians to possess

character traits that go by the same names as the Christian-style virtues. But when a person possesses these traits in the peculiarly Christian way—that is, in a way that legitimizes the title "fruits of the Holy Spirit"—then that person possesses them as an imitator of God. They are reflections of the Persons in whose home and presence the Christian dwells. The Christian does not—at least ideally—live by stated *rules*; the Christian lives instead by having a certain kind of *mind*, namely, the mind of Christ. That person "has a mind" to nurture the poor and abandoned, to forgive those who offend against oneself, to treat all persons gently; and that mind is not one's own but the mind of the Lord with whom one daily communes. By this communing with God in prayerful meditation, the Christian has cottoned on to God's style. A boy who loves and admires his father (and also lives with him) cottons on, in ways beyond his ability to articulate, to his father's style of doing things. The child does not say, "Dad does it this way, so I will do it this way too." He just imbibes his father's style. God too has a style, and Christians who love him and dwell in his presence will find themselves, after a while, reflecting it.

I have emphasized the congregation of God's people as a central context in which spirituality is nurtured, because Christian spirituality is intercourse, and it is in the congregation that God's Spirit is present in a special way. But there are, sadly, congregations in which the spirit or spirits that are moving do not engender God's styles of gentleness, forgiveness, nurturing of the poor and abandoned, and kindness to one's enemies. Instead, we may find the styles of dissension, self-righteousness, punishment of enemies, and sometimes even racial bigotry. People can sometimes fellowship for years in such a place, without suffering the faintest press to be colored by the styles of God. But such a congregation is gathered only in the name—not in the Spirit—of Jesus. Whether people are likely, upon associating with a congregation, to be infected with the styles of Jesus is a mark of the faithfulness of that congregation.

The Strengths

To a third group of spiritual traits often mentioned in the New Testament I have given the name of "strengths." In this list belong such fruits of the Spirit as steadfastness, self-control, patience, perseverance, and courage. These traits are neither emotions nor styles of behavior. If you know, for example, that somebody is steadfast, but don't know anything else about that person, then you don't have any clue, as yet, as to how he or she feels or behaves; all you know is that *however* he or she feels and behaves, there is a kind of regularity and persistence and steadiness in behavior. That is, whatever the person's spirituality is, you can count on its being exhibited even in situations that might militate against it. You can count on it to resist the temptations that come from boredom, threats, anxiety, pleasures, and social pressures. The steadfast person is not easily derailed from a committed life; the commitment *means* something. What is integrity? Originally, the word denoted "the ability to stay together." To have integrity is to remain an entirety. Hard, strong, well-structured things have integrity; you can push them around, pull on them, and jerk them, and they don't fall apart or lose their shape. And the Christian is like that: hard at the center, tough, not blown about by every wind of doctrine, not put off course by threats from enemies; not a chameleon, changing color according to the environment.

Now to follow through with this metaphor of the Christian character as having both a shape and the strength to retain that shape, we can say that what provides the shape of the Christian character is the emotions and the styles, while "steadfastness," "patience," "courage," and so forth are names for the toughness by which the Christian retains hope, compassion, gentleness, and gratitude. When I compared being in the spirit of Christmas with being in the spirit of Socrates, I emphasized that the former was a kind of passing mood, while the latter was a deep infection. The former occurs when the individual is in a certain kind of environment, while the latter is environmentally independent. When the biblical writers stress steadfastness so strongly, they are saying that the hope, compassion, gentleness, and gratitude of the Christian spirit are not moods that can appropriately pass when the last note of the organ stops sounding, or the Bible study group disperses to individual homes, or when persecutions set in or the temptations of the flesh beckon. Christian spirituality is not a state of mood but a state of character.

Ideally, the strengths are nothing but an *aspect* of the emotions and styles. That is, they are just the fact that the Christian's hope and gentleness and gratitude are deep and tough. Ideally, one should not need to talk about steadfastness, but just about hope and gentleness and the like. I say "ideally," because in most of us the Christian emotions and styles are pretty shaky. Presumably this was true also of first-century Christians, and explains why the New Testament writers so often exhort their readers to patience and perseverance. But since we are so shaky, it is fitting to talk about the strengths of a Christian, as well as emotions and styles of behavior, and to reflect about what these strengths are and how they can be cultivated. This, like the other fruits of the Spirit, is a fitting theme for pastors and other spiritual guides to apply themselves to, for the upbuilding of the church to the measure of the stature of the fullness of Christ, so that we may no longer be children, tossed to and fro, but grow up in every way into him who is the head, into Christ. Three of the strengths of the Christian are the subject of this book.

CHAPTER TWO
SELF-CONTROL

Who has a harder struggle than he who labors to conquer himself? This ought to be our endeavor, to conquer ourselves, and daily to wax stronger than ourselves, and to make some progress for good.
Thomas à Kempis
The Imitation of Christ

Self-control and the "Self"

People struggle with, and sometimes gain mastery of, not only physical nature, machines, intellectual problems, and each other but also *themselves*. When you begin to think about it, the idea of struggling with yourself, and of mastering yourself, may appear strange. Are there two selves inside you, the one that gets mastered and the one that does the mastering? But this cannot be, for if there are really two selves, then we no longer have *one* person controlling the *self* but rather the control of one person by another. So when you control yourself it is not like pinning your identical twin until he says "uncle."

In the summer of 1982 my family and I went to live in Holland for three months. The cultural contrast between America and Holland is not very great if you compare it with that between, say, America and New Guinea, or even Iran. And I had my family, including my Dutch-immigrant wife, with me. But even with these advantages, I had the vague anxious sensation, during the first few weeks, of *wondering who I was*. The woman in whose house we were living spoke only Dutch, so all the household conversation went on in a language I could barely understand and speak even less well. My role became one of much greater dependency than I am used to at home. While I was not tempted to respond to this with bizarre behavior my experience did have one thing in common with experiences of temptation. The edge had been taken off the solid sense of my own identity. My sense of self was there, all right, below the surface of my disorientation, but it felt threatened. Something similar happens when we are significantly tempted: We see the temptation as something alien to our deepest or realest self (if we didn't, it would not be temptation) and as something that threatens to encroach upon that self and to displace it or dissolve it.

The concept of self-control verges on metaphor; what is dominated is not literally yourself, at least not your deepest self, but something that was vying to *become* a part of you, something that the real you considers extraneous and unwelcome. The justification, however, for that little word "self" in the expression "self-control" is that that extraneous element is too close to your real self for comfort. It is like barnacles, which adhere so tightly to the ship that they might be mistaken for a part of it (they actually have to be scraped off). However, the relationship between the threatening "self" that gets controlled and your real self is more fluid than that between barnacles and a ship. The barnacles never actually become part of the ship, but if you are not on your guard and active in self-control, your "self"—that extraneous element which needs to be scraped away—may indeed become part of the real you.

What is this extraneous element, too close to the self for comfort, which a person manages in self-control? It is inclinations directed at ends that are at odds with our perceived spiritual and prudential ends. Sometimes they are momentary *impulses*, like the gluttonous urge to take one more piece of cake, or the angry impulse to strike a child. Sometimes they are *feelings*, like twinges of envy or impatience, contempt or revulsion, which are at odds with our more considered sense of how we ought to regard other people. Sometimes they are passionate *attachments*: a compulsion like gambling, or an erotic captivation that must not be allowed to take its course. Often they are a mixture of impulse, emotion, and passion. But they all share in common that they are adversaries, in some sense, of what we more deeply conceive ourselves to be, or ought to be. To give in to them is to suffer damage to our selves.

But that nobler me, if it has begun to develop somewhat deeply, is not just an ideal picture of what I ought to be. It is itself composed of passions, compulsions, captivations, enthusiasms, and interests—and consequently of impulses and emotions. The self of the Christian, for example, is composed of love for God and his kingdom and thus for the neighbor as coinhabitant of God's kingdom. The emotions of joy and hope and contrition and the impulses of compassion and mercy and gentleness will be frequent episodes of the Christian's conscious life. Thus self-control is not a power of rooting out all impulses, emotions, and passions whatsoever. Instead it is a delicate and sometimes playful power of weeding—of uprooting *some* passions so that others may grow to maturity, blossom, and bear fruit. It is out of interest in the kingdom of God that the Christian most characteristically controls the self. But, on the other hand, it is only because this interest is not overwhelming—because other, adverse, interests are strong enough to be threateningly competitive with the passion for the kingdom of God— that the Christian needs self-control. If my best self—my kingdom self—were fully formed and I had all my "priorities" straight, I would not need self-control.

Self-control and Behavior-control

We must distinguish between real *self*-control and mere *behavior*-control. True self-control is the successful management of your impulses, emotions, concerns, wants, passions, and the like. It is not merely the suppression or mitigation of the behavior in which these inclinations threaten to issue, but the suppression or modification of the inclinations themselves. Later we will see that important strategies for altering our inclinations involve performing overt actions, since just the right kind of actions in the appropriate circumstances can cause our inclinations to change; but this fact leaves the distinction between inclination-control and behavior-control intact.

There are gradations between mere behavior-control and real self-control, but for the sake of starkness let me illustrate with a case where behavior-control though self-initiated is just about as mere as it can be. Let's say I'm fat and threatened with a heart attack. In a moment of terror I sit down and think: I do a lot of my eating directly out of the refrigerator; if I could just stop *that*, I'd probably cut my calories by half. I buy a chain and padlock, run the chain through the door handle, loop it tightly around the fridge, lock it and give the key to my wife, with absolute instructions never to tell me where it is. Thus I blockade my eating behavior. I do not seek to alter my *attitude* toward food, so as to weaken or dissipate the impulse to eat at inappropriate times, but only seek to ensure, by manipulating the circumstances, that my behavior will be thwarted. This strategy is not *self*-control. I have in no way changed my patterns of impulse, my likes and dislikes, my attitudes and interests and emotions.

Think now of the contrasting kind of case. Instead of asking myself the rather crass question "How can I keep myself from eating so much?" I ask, "What do I *see* in food that I should feel so compelled to congest myself with it at all hours of day and night?" As a result of reflecting about myself over a period of time in the context of the struggle and the inevitable failures (and maybe an occasional success), I come, perhaps, to a hypothesis about myself. I notice that I perceive food largely as a form of *wealth* and a source of *security*. I'm a little like a miser, fondling money and fondly stashing it away, checking frequently to make sure it's still there. Of course, food tastes good, but to myself I seem to want more from it than culinary pleasure: I get a perverse feeling of well-being when taking food into myself, quite apart from the hunger I feel (I almost never feel hungry, in the strict sense) or the pleasure it gives me. My comfort is like the feeling of pushing my burdened cart through the checkout aisle at the market, or putting my paycheck in the bank. I think to myself, "Now, there, I'm O.K. for a while." Like all forms of greedy wealth-gathering, this one weighs me down. Instead of the security I seek, I get enslavement and misery.

If I begin to see things this way, then self-control becomes a different, and deeper, challenge. It is really a challenge to my passions and attitudes, the *meaning* food has for me. Just seeing what the root of my problem is—greed and the fixation on food as a source of security—may have some tendency to free me from it. But it is unlikely that mere insight will bring about the desired change in my self. I must *remember* that insight at appropriate moments, must *dwell* on that insight while gazing upon food I am free to pick up and eat. I must work on my vision, much as someone works on a tennis serve.

I might try fasting for a day, or several days, not so much with a view to losing weight as for a time of meditation on the significance of food in my life. And during the fast, which heightens my appreciation of food but also asserts a certain degree of independence from it, I reflect on relevant Bible passages, perhaps on Jesus' discourse on the lilies and the birds (Matt. 6:26, 28): "Is not life more than food?" Or on the concept of manna (Ex. 16:31), the food which *God* provided for just the *day*. All food is, after all, really manna: a good gift from on high, to be received, as the birds receive it, gladly but without hoarding or possessing. Or I might use the Lord's Prayer, "Give us this day our daily bread," attempting to let God burn into my consciousness the futility and perversity of trying to collect food in my stomach. If I succeed in getting a more just vision of food, then I will also have succeeded, in some small way, in transferring the weight of my trust from such idols to the great God who is the source of all good things.

Such meditative acts will tend to give me resources for keeping my cool in the presence of food, memories to call into play when temptations arise. The "meditation" must not be restricted to quiet times and Bible-readings, for part of the struggle against gluttony is to learn to see this *particular* food, steaming on the plate before me, as manna, the good gift of sustenance from God, which cannot be hoarded and must be received in due measure. I need to be able to look down at that pork chop and see in it not wealth but God's sustaining gift to me for this occasion, to experience not greed but gratitude. To eat gratefully is to eat in moderation; to eat with greed and anxiety is to eat immoderately. The struggle to see it in this way is *self*-struggle, and the success in which it may issue is *self*-control.

Basic Self-control

I have not meant to imply that everyone who has an eating problem (as almost all of us do—including the slender ones) regards food primarily as wealth. Some regard it as a means of punishing their parents, others more or less as a way of getting pleasure, still others as a means of asserting their superiority, and there are no doubt numerous other perverse ways of regarding it. My example is not meant to suggest a theory of gluttony but to illustrate the distinction between true self-struggle, which aims to master adverse impulses and inclinations and their deeper sources, and the kind of struggle which, superficially, thinks the main job is getting one's behavior under control.

One of my proposals is that the strength-virtues are, for a large part of their range, *capacities* that we can learn by practice. And very often these capacities are skills for managing adverse inclinations, impulses, moods, habits, and emotions. Quite often, as in the above illustration, these skills, like athletic ones, involve the use of strategy. The skilled tennis player has not only motor skills but also the capacity to frame (usually with lightning speed) strategies for dealing with an opponent and for correcting error. The fact that urges to eat and perverse attitudes toward food take many forms points up that such strategies have to be tailored to the individual. Meditating on the nature of food as manna might not be at all strategic for somebody who overate as a way of getting revenge on his or her parents. Here some other strategy of self-control would probably be called for.

Thus self-control, like the other strength-virtues, has a component of self-knowledge in it. Often you have to have a pretty clear understanding of the inner adversities you are up against before you can devise ways of altering them or heading them off. But I must also emphasize that this self-knowledge is not the kind that issues primarily in *insights* or *pronouncements* about yourself. If we were to distinguish between knowing-that (information or insight about oneself) and knowing-how, the kind of self-knowledge we are talking about here would definitely be a sort of self-know-*how*. You cannot have it without having a certain amount of insight about yourself, but insight is not enough; you also have to know how to *manage* yourself.

Now, having said that self-control is often strategic and involves practical acquaintance with the special bumps and recesses in your own psyche, I want to mention an aspect of self-control of which this is probably not true, a kind of *basic* self-control which, if we hesitate to call a skill, we can at least still call a power. William James, one of our century's first psychologists, gives the following advice:

> Keep the faculty of effort alive in you by a little gratuitous exercise every day. That is, be systematically ascetic or heroic in little unnecessary points, do every day or two something for no other reason than that you would rather not do it, so that when the hour of dire need draws nigh, it may find you not unnerved and untrained to stand the test.

Thus if you want a helping of dessert, though you have no reason to refuse it, refuse it as a little practice in resisting desires. Your eye is drawn to the pretty woman across the street; refuse the eye its pleasure as an act of ascetic discipline. If you practice this sort of thing regularly, suggests James, your will will be strengthened; you will be more the master of yourself.

If it is true, as it seems to be, that we can gain a *general* power over our desires and impulses by practicing the denial of them, then this too will be an important part of self-control. Here the "power" that self-control amounts to is more literally a strength than is the strategic kind that I have been discussing hitherto. It is like a spiritual muscularity. And I would think that any Christian would want to be equipped with this kind of strength, for when bad impulses beset us—and they are bound to do so until we become perfect saints—it will be useful to be able to dispatch them, not only by refined strategies such as meditation on the spiritual significance of food but also by simply muscling them aside for the moment.

This latter sort of impulse mastery also belongs in the category of genuine self-control as contrasted with mere behavior-control, insofar as the strength gained through asceticism means that the impulse itself becomes a relatively less powerful force in one's life.

Spiritual and Nonspiritual Self-control

Our second distinction is between spiritual and nonspiritual self-control. People can have all sorts of motives and mixtures thereof for struggling with themselves. I mentioned that our overweight person was threatened with heart attack, but this individual might also have wanted to cut the grocery bill, or trim down to the size of last year's wardrobe, or avoid embarrassment, or become a more effective sales representative, or be fit for athletics, or impress others by increased self-control. I think we can agree that self-control exercised for these ends, though possibly genuine, is not *spiritual*.

I have pointed out that self-control is made genuine by its being a control of our inclinations rather than merely of our behavior; it is made spiritual by being exercised out of a spiritual motive. A Christian might believe that, quite independently of considerations of fat and health, it is important to see and treat food as manna. Such a way of seeing is part of being the kind of person you want to be, a person tuned to your nature as a child of God. Even if your metabolism can burn off calories fast enough to keep your body slim, and even if no one is going to raise an eyebrow at the sight of food shoveling, still you feel an obligation, out of love for God and respect for yourself, to eat like the birds of the air—not with greed or a sense of possession, but in the silent gratitude of freedom before your Maker, taking what is needed for the moment.

Three times our Lord instructs us (Matt. 6:2, 5, 16) to hide our good actions from public view (he gives as examples praying, giving to the poor, and fasting); "and your Father who sees in secret," he says, "will reward you." Jesus is not equating the "inner" with the spiritual and the "outer" with the worldly; instead, he is proposing the use of "secrecy" as a way of coping with our worldliness. He also instructs us to pray, "Lead us not into temptation," and I would venture to say that hiding our goodness is a way of avoiding temptation. How great is the temptation, when other people are applauding us for some goodness, to take joy in the applause rather than in the goodness! And how great is the temptation to open ourselves to this temptation by orchestrating the situations of our goodness for maximum visibility! But these temptations are very serious in Jesus' view. About people who do good with a view to applause, he says, "they have received their reward," implying that their taking joy in the applause is incompatible with the spiritual joy that is God's reward. Since they regard with such enthusiasm the applause they receive from their fellows, they will *not* have the reward of becoming true persons before God.

Self-struggle is by no means the special domain of Christians. People of all stripes and many motives will find importance in genuine self-control. But the Christian has a kind of standard—a spiritual one—which persons of most other stripes do not consider and which indeed, to their eyes, may look like foolishness. For in the struggles with self, Christians seek first not to get ahead in the world or to win the world's praise but to become persons fit to live transparently to themselves and in the view of the all-seeing secret eye of the Holy One.

The Case of Etty Hillesum

Etty Hillesum was a remarkable young Jewish Dutch woman whose diary for the years 1941–1943 has recently been published. It is rich in psychological self-analysis, and particularly in the description of her emotional struggles. One of the chief struggles of the early pages concerns her relationship with an older man of attractive and commanding personality, Julius Spier. For several reasons, she wishes to become free from her feelings of attachment to him. At one point she writes:

> I have again become a little bit stronger. I can fight it out with the things that are going on in me. First you are inclined to go get help from somebody else, to think: "I'm not making it," but all at once you notice that you've again fought something through and that you've pulled it off on your own and that makes you even stronger. Last Sunday (just a week ago) I had the desperate feeling that I was irrevocably bound to him and that a dreadfully unhappy period was in store for me. But I jerked myself loose, only I don't understand how. Not by reasoning with myself about the matter. But I pulled with all my psychic might on an imaginary rope, I resisted and exerted myself and suddenly I felt that I was free again. . . .
>
> I would just like to know *how* I did it, that pulling loose. It's a process that's not yet clear to me. I have to get clear about it so that later perhaps I can help others who have the same difficulty. Perhaps I can best compare it with someone who is bound to another with a rope and jerks and pulls so long that he gets loose. He himself would perhaps not be able to say later how he got loose, he just knows that he

had the *will* to get loose, and that he applied all his powers to it. Psychically that seems to be how it went with me. Here is something else I learned from the experience: reasoning things out doesn't help, making it clear to oneself what's what and looking for causes: one simply has to do something psychical, to expend energy to get a result. (Pp. 32f.)

When we struggle with ourselves we sometimes succeed, and yet almost always without having any very clear idea why we succeeded this time but failed at some other time. Etty Hillesum seems to regard self-struggle as an activity that can be gone about more or less intelligently; thus one who knew *what she was doing* would have an advantage and be able to instruct others. I think her image is useful. All of us, unless we are self-indulgent slobs, have a rough-and-ready, intuitive, practical grasp of self-management, just as we know that sometimes pulling on a rope will make it come loose. But if we knew more about the kind of knot at the other end, and thus had a basis for developing the skill of jiggling and tugging and flipping the rope so as to facilitate the loosening of the knot, our efforts at self-mastery would become more fruitful. And in turn we might become encouraged by our success to exert ourselves still further, as Etty Hillesum was, and thus with further practice to deepen our self-mastery.

Throughout this book I will try to clarify the adversities against which we struggle with ourselves, to investigate the nature of our impulses, habits, emotions, and attachments for clues as to how they can be managed. The answers to this question vary according to the contexts in which we ask it. Etty Hillesum says that "reasoning things out doesn't help, making clear to oneself what's what and looking for causes," but it seems clear that she is speaking of her *own* case in that particular moment of struggle. She had tried investigating the nature and causes of her attachment to Spier and had made some headway, but this reflection didn't free her from the attachment. When all was said and thought, she simply had to "pull" herself loose from him. (By the way, this is by no means the end of the struggle for her as recorded in the diary.) But the cases are not always so; sometimes thinking through an attachment or impulse *is* sufficient for freeing oneself from it. As soon as one takes a hard look at it, it loses all appeal. So the cases are mixed. Sometimes reflection is enough (though you may have to force yourself to reflect honestly and vividly). Sometimes you have to perform an act of resignation, to decide to see things in a different way. Sometimes nothing short of performing some action, making some gesture, setting yourself in a demanding or dangerous situation, will alter your susceptibility to the inclination in question.

Etty Hillesum is an "intellectual," and we might speculate that the reason thinking through her attachment failed to change her attitude is to be found here. Because of the intellectual's frequently practiced skill in thinking things through, the thinking tends to get detached from personal concerns. Intellectual training tends to make people capable of self-construals which, however insightful, are nevertheless spiritually superficial. They remain in a "detached," experimental attitude, so that their thoughts tend not to grip them emotionally. What Etty needed in order to break loose from Spier emotionally was to see with her *heart*, to *appreciate* the inappropriateness of the relationship, to bring herself to perceive its repugnant facets. As long as she was just playing intellectual games of psychoanalysis on herself and Spier, she was only doing the spadework and was not yet down to serious emotional gardening.

Often, more drastic measures than mere reflection are needed if a person is to change emotional responses to things. (Right emotions are, in general, a more important and difficult achievement than right thoughts—though you can't have right emotions without having thoughts that are at least in the right ballpark.) In the episode she describes, Etty Hillesum seems to have become *willing*, at least for the moment, to see Spier in a certain light; and although she would perhaps never have seen him in this light if she had not had certain thoughts about him ("making it clear to oneself what's what"), the thoughts did not go so far as to become ingredients in her emotions until she had done "something psychical," something that can be described, vaguely, like this: to *let* herself be *touched* by what was repugnant in the relationship.

Reflecting about the remarks from Etty Hillesum seems to confirm three points that emerged earlier in our discussion. First, self-control is a sort of *know-how*, something a person can practice, learn, and improve in over time. Second, improving your self-control seems to involve an increase in self-knowledge; so we can speculate that part of the know-how of self-control is, as with other kinds of know-how, *insight* concerning what you are about, what you are up against (in this case the adversities against which you set yourself in self-struggle). And the third point follows from the second: Self-control is something you must learn for yourself, not just because nobody can learn a skill for you, but because self-control is in its nature an ability that must be adapted to a *particular* self, which in significant ways may differ from other selves. In the following sections I shall discuss the Christian's control of anger, hoping that these points will become more vivid and practical.

The Hillbilly and the Coward

Let me begin with a story. A man I'll call Philip lived in a bright-blue house smack between a gray one to the north and a white one to the south. This put Philip in the middle—in more than one way, as will soon be apparent. Philip owned the blue and the gray houses, and as time went by he rented the gray one to a family with three children. The children were of racially mixed parentage, with a white mother and a black father, but did not let the question of color deter them from becoming the best of friends with Philip's little son Nathanael. In the white house to the south lived an older couple who had moved into town some years earlier, in retirement from a farm in the country. They also had become quite attached to Nathanael, who from his side had come to recognize the white house as an inexhaustible source of Jell-O.

The old man had declared to Philip over the hedge on a couple of occasions, "I haven't got anything against black folk [pause] . . . Don't trust 'em." Another time he said the one question he had asked before bidding on the house was whether there were any blacks on the block. When the block had been given a clean bill of health, he bought the house. He passed on to Philip stories (which seemed to be making their way up and down the block) about the illegitimate pregnancy that had eventuated in the first of the children, the peeping-Tom activities of the father, and other such stories. At these recitations Philip, who was not much of a crusader by nature, bit his tongue and usually tried to change the subject. The old man's words angered him all right, but it was a cool anger, with an admixture of good-humored indulgence for an old hillbilly who didn't know any better. (He did know better.)

But one afternoon the old man motioned Philip over to the rock fence that separated their backyards and pointed to a green gate which had formerly been lying askew, allowing free passage by little feet from one yard to the other. He had wired it tightly upright, and in tones of hushed familiarity he explained that it was there to keep the black children off his premises. He hastened to add, reassuringly, that Nathanael was as welcome as ever. The blatancy of the old man's racism, the repulsiveness to Philip of having his son singularly favored for no better reason than the color of his skin, and the implication, by the tones of hushed confidence, that he would certainly sympathize with the old man's worry about the "pollution" of his yard, suddenly terminated Philip's period of tongue-biting. His sense of indulgent good humor about the old man's backward ways began to look to him like a case of moral complacency, and he gave his heart leave to be engulfed in anger. In a raised voice he called his neighbor a bigot and a racist and informed him that he was in defiance of the love of Jesus and in disobedience of the will of God. (These theological facts seemed relevant, since the man was an obedient member of his church, priding himself that potable alcohol had never touched his lips.) Seeing the ire in Philip's eyes, the old man declared he wouldn't borrow Philip's ladders any more and, thinking to get revenge with a Bible verse, quoted Paul: "Be angry but do not sin; do not let the sun go down on your anger." The vengeance was of course ill-conceived, since the verse does not condemn anger, only letting the sun go down on it. Philip accepted the advice.

Anger, Judgment, and Hatred

Anger is an emotion that may stem from the worst as well as the best of orientations. Both the outlook and the concern that it evinces may range from the purest, as when Jesus looks with anger on the pinched and ungodly piety of those who would disapprove healing on the Sabbath for a crippled man (Mark 3), to the very despicable, as when a racist-nationalist is angered by the hiring of Southeast Asians for jobs that could be done by white Americans. Unlike the related emotion of hatred, anger directed toward persons is not, as such, bad; before we can determine whether it is, we must look at the individual case. There *is* such a thing as righteous indignation.

But the Christian is cautious about anger. For the cases of genuine righteousness in it are pretty rare, and even when some righteousness cleaves to it, pitfalls abound. Obviously, anger is misguided when it is based on some *false* judgment—for example, when you are angry at somebody for doing something that person didn't do, or for doing something that could not be avoided in the circumstances, or angry at a child for doing something the child could not be expected to have the knowledge or self-mastery to refrain from. These are the most blatant and easily corrigible cases of wrongful anger. But there are deeper reasons for the Christian's caution about anger.

Foremost is that anger implies judgment and the inclination toward vengeance. It is a strongly *moralizing* emotion. To the person toward whom I am angry, I say, as it were: "You have offended in a way that merits punishment. Maybe I am not in a position to mete out the punishment you deserve; but I stand here as your judge and would gladly also fill the role of executioner, if that were my good fortune." Even when we are angry with someone we love for doing something that offends only against his or her self, there are still these elements of moral judgment and the desire to punish. If this seems untrue, I submit that you are not thinking of a case in which you are genuinely angry with a person you love.

Because judgment and vengeance are ingredients in anger, the Christian ought not to approve anger unqualifiedly even when it is justified by the behavior of the offending person. For there is something deeply unfitting about me, a sinner, playing this role of judge and avenger. True, I cannot, in all clarity, not know that the offender has offended. But I *can* refrain from dwelling on the guilt, and certainly I can refrain from punishing the person. And it is appropriate, in the overwhelming majority of cases, that I do refrain from such invidious attention to another's shortcomings and from punishing with accusing words or sour glances, with avoidance of that person's company or withholding of affection, or perhaps some even crasser form of punishment. Our anger tends to be perpetuated by our enjoyment of it; and our enjoyment seems to stem from the sense of moral superiority we gain from clothing ourselves in judges' robes. But when we do so we offend perhaps more despicably than the one we judge, for we have forgotten our own status as sinner and tried to usurp the place of God, to whom alone vengeance belongs.

Paul did not condemn anger as such, but he did advise not to let the sun go down on it. In these two facts we see reflected two truths about anger. First, no person with ethical passion can avoid anger for long, for occasions of it abound in a world of darkness such as we inhabit. Never to experience anger is to be without character. But second, the kind of burning vengefulness that Philip felt toward the old bigot is not a state in which a person ought to dwell. I have already noted that anger, if too fully owned, tends to usurp the role of God. But in human beings anger can lead to a degeneration of the self. We speak of brooding anger and grudge bearing, and we talk about people being "consumed" by anger. The word "consumed" is precise. We can imagine Philip dwelling, day after day and week after week, upon the unrighteousness of his neighbor. And his focus, if he does this, will tend to become not the offense that the neighbor has committed, or the suffering that the neighbor's offense has brought upon others, but the neighbor himself as wicked and worthy of harm. As the sun sets and the anger abides, the anger degenerates into hatred and the self of gentleness and compassion and mercy is consumed. A person with habitual and long-term angers will be not just angry but also hateful; and to hate other persons is to suffer moral death.

The case of anger that I have made the centerpiece of our discussion is a righteous one, not only in that it takes a morally right perspective but also in the added sense that the perspective is relatively disinterested. If Philip were the black man and his child the one excluded by the green gate, then we would have a case of self-interested anger. This is perhaps the more common form that "righteous indignation" takes. This kind of anger, though righteous, is perhaps even more dangerous, for the danger of brooding is larger here. Most people are more exercised about their own rights than about those of others; and those who do possess the greatness of soul to be concerned about the rights of others are made likely, by this very trait, to have a large enough perspective on their angers to prevent them from becoming grudges. Further, what is required is forgiveness, a very difficult matter; whereas it would be fatuous, as well as obscene, for Philip to *forgive* the old bigot. The place where anger is most likely to degenerate into hatred, and thus become soul consuming, is in familial relationships: a younger brother nurses resentment against his elder sibling into old age for high-handed injustices suffered in their youth; one son begrudges his mother, beyond her dying day, the preferential treatment she gave his brother; a wife, divorced unjustly, refuses to let her anger float out upon the boundless waters but cherishes it, stinking, in the harbor of her heart.

Controlling Anger

What is it to "control" anger? We are not speaking merely of mitigating or masking its behavior symptoms. Philip resolved not to let the sun go down on his anger. But he will not have succeeded if the next morning he puts on a friendly countenance toward his neighbor while hoping in his secret heart that the old man will fall over his shovel and impale himself on his rake. So our question is: "How do you mitigate the anger itself?" One very widespread answer to the question is: "Find some way to blow off steam." The theory behind this answer is that anger is internal pressure, like the air inside a tire. If this is so, then the only way to get rid of it is to *let it out*. Thus Philip could get rid of his anger at the old man by jumping over the hedge and punching him in the nose, or by inviting twenty of his black friends to a party on the front lawn. Or if he wanted to divert the blowing steam of his anger away from his neighbor he might yell at his wife or Nathanael or set fire to his own garage.

Fortunately, the pressure-theory of anger is false. The kernel of truth in it is that anger can be *satisfied*, and when it is thoroughly satisfied it disappears. I have already remarked that anger includes the desire to punish somebody for an offense; and presumably Philip could get rid of his anger by thoroughly drubbing the old man, or by doing something else to make himself feel that matters had been set to rights. But if Philip used this method to get rid of his anger, we would surely not call him *self-controlled*. Self-control is not getting rid of your anger in just any way you please.

Real self-control, in connection with anger, is a matter of bringing yourself to see the old man in a nonangry, or coolly angry, light, for emotions are ways of seeing things. As I pointed out in connection with Etty Hillesum, what works for one person may not work for another, and the learning of self-control is, in all its aspects, to some extent a matter of reckoning with the peculiarities of your own psyche and developing skills of self-mastery tailored to them. We can, however, venture some suggestions which may have some value generally, if not universally, and which, even if not directly applicable to everyone, may spark some useful insights.

To be hotly angry with somebody is to focus on that person in a particular way: as an offender (against yourself or someone else) and thus as worthy of punishment. It is also to see yourself indirectly as an appropriate judge of the case, and most likely also as an appropriate punisher, insofar as you are inclined toward punishing behavior. (I say indirectly because the focus is not on you; you are a presupposed background of this focus.) So most control of anger is, in one way or another, a matter of altering your focus on the person you are angry with, or your understanding of yourself, or both.

The simple expedient of counting to ten before expressing your anger is quite effective. And the reason it sometimes works is that, especially if the anger is subrational, the counting and the waiting tend to cause you to take a different view of the situation. If you give yourself time, perhaps you will see that you are not in a position to judge the other, or it will occur to you that there may be another side to the story than the one that seemed so compelling in the heat of the moment, or you may come to see that the person really did not offend at all! On the other hand, if you fly off the handle, lodging your head in the other's viscera, you are likely to sustain your anger and even deepen it. For to *behave* as a judge and punisher is to confirm yourself in that view of yourself and to confirm your view of the other as an offender. Besides, the other person may well retaliate, and then you *will* have cause to be angry.

The fact that angry behavior confirms you in anger suggests another way of controlling anger. For you can also change your focus on the other person by engaging in some overt behavior that is incompatible with anger. For example, let us say that your wife has done something that irritates you: She has come home from work an hour late without calling, and the children have been beastly all afternoon, and you have been eagerly awaiting a little relief and adult companionship. It seems she got to drinking wine with some of her business friends and lost track of the time. She is apologetic, but you find yourself seething and inclined in all sorts of ways to get revenge; to be sullen, to withhold affection, to burn the carrots, to remark sarcastically on how nice it must be to relax with friends. But instead of "expressing" yourself in any of these ways, you quite intentionally act contrary to your anger: You take her in your arms, kiss her tenderly, look at her with the intention of seeing the beloved gift God has given you for a companion, and say "I love you." It is better *not* to say, "It's good to have you home," or "The kids and I have really been looking forward to seeing you," or anything else that you or she might interpret as sarcastic, even if you're trying not to be, because this is a slippery moment, when things can easily go bad. But if you can manage to behave in a way that is strongly incompatible with your anger, you will find that very often it disappears. And the reason is that in behaving this way you make it difficult for yourself to see her as offensive or to cast yourself for yourself in the role of judge and punisher.

Likewise if you are Philip, wishing to bring it about that the sun does not go down on your anger toward the old bigot next door, you will want to see yourself and him in a different light than you did in the heat of the encounter. Perhaps you will want to go to a quiet place and meditate on some of the concrete similarities between yourself and the old man: The forms of *your* bigotry, present and former, the pride by which *you*, like him, set yourself without warrant above other children of God. If you can bring yourself to see these things vividly, your own role as judge and punisher, necessary to anger, will fade away. And on the other side, reflect on the old man. Who is he, after all? A sinner, yes, like you, but is he not also one for whom Christ died? I said it would be ludicrous for Philip to forgive him his sin against the family of five; but there is after all a way in which Philip, without forgiving the old man, can participate emotionally in God's forgiveness of him and thus drive the anger from his heart before the sun goes down. For he can remember that while we were yet sinners, hating God and hating and harming one another, Christ died for the ungodly; and he can remember that that old bigot with the fury in his eye is one of those lost sheep the Good Shepherd came to rescue.

CHAPTER THREE
PATIENCE

How much interior emigration there is all about us! Students emigrate to the future. . . . Displaced persons live in the past. . . . Parents are . . . living for the day when the children are raised, or when they will retire . . . , but remain numb and glazed and absent from the living moment.

Douglas V. Steere
On Being Present Where You Are

Why Patience Is a Virtue

The apostle Paul says love is patient, and I would like to suggest that in this life patience is something like a girder of love. Just as a girder gives a building inner strength against the weights and winds and possible earthquakes that it must bear, so patience is a kind of strengthening or adversity-resisting factor that makes love possible when it is difficult. You need patience with all the objects of Christian love: God, your neighbor, and yourself. Let us start with a general account.

Patience is the ability to dwell gladly in the present moment when we have some desire, or what would normally be a reason to desire, to depart from it. It is not necessarily connected with love. It takes patience to be a good duck hunter or scholar or even a good thief. Waiting for the ducks to come near the blind may get boring, just as reading some theologians may be. So you might say that patience is not only a girder of love but also of a lot of other human endeavors as well—good and bad and neutral. Patience is not only a Christian virtue but a virtue in the book of anybody who understands a bit about human life. There are three reasons for this.

First, our life is full of beckonings from the future: The future (one form of that delicious-looking grass in the other pasture) says, "Come away from where you are; you are not moving fast enough, not accomplishing enough, not getting what you set out to get. And is it not a bit boring where you are, and unpleasant and annoying in other ways? Come away, come away." And so the craftsman rushes his job, or the scholar lays aside the volume of Moltmann's theology, or the pastor gives up on a hard case in the parish and maybe thinks about going into counseling or teaching or sewage administration. Some people are so deficient in patience that they flit from task to task or from entertainment to entertainment, never doing anything well or enjoying anything deeply. Patience is a form of self-mastery that enables us to dwell in the present moment, to stay at the present task, to narrow our focus of vision so that our mind is not sundered by every passing impulse to quit the present and fly away. And as such it is a necessary condition for the *accomplishment* of anything worthwhile.

Second, patience is a condition for *happiness*. Some vices are enjoyable, or at least seem so at the moment when you are practicing them. For example, most people get a delicious pleasure out of invidious gossip. But other vices are just thoroughly unpleasant. Envy, for example, is evil through and through but at the same time a beastly pain. You can imagine some pretty normal people looking for a chance to gossip or commit adultery, but somebody would have to be crazy to go looking for an opportunity to be envious.

Impatience is a constitutionally unpleasant vice. It is a state of more or less intense *frustration:* you want to be somewhere other, or doing something other, or accomplishing something other, or in the company of someone other, than you are. Some people's impatience is limited to certain moments, but other people are beset with impatience about large segments and pervasive situations of their life: for example, the minister who hates the small-town congregation he is pastoring and is just living for the day when he will be able to move on to greener pastures; or the mother of small children who just can't wait until they grow up enough to go to school and get out of her hair. These are ones whose impatience has made them unhappy people, rather than just people with unhappy moments. By contrast, people who can dwell gladly in the present moment despite some desire, or what would normally be a reason to desire, to depart from it—are not frustrated. Because they exercise patience, this present moment of life is something in which to rejoice and be glad. The impulses to flee are under control, and they experience peace and self-acceptance.

But patience is not just a condition for accomplishment and happiness; in the third place, it is also a condition for the integration of the person. It is part of what it takes to become what the philosopher Søren Kierkegaard calls a "single individual"; or the poet John Keats calls being a "soul"; or the Quaker George Fox calls being an "established man." Like the other strengths, patience gives our lives continuity and autonomy, enabling us to live not by impulse, or at the rude beck and call of environmental stimulus, but by some design. Whether the particular design is worthy of a human self is another question; but even if a person's life project is making money or gaining fame, patience will be required for the activities and the resulting accomplishments to be in a deeper sense that *person's*.

The Christian design is of course the love of God and neighbor.

> Someone asked Abba Anthony, "What must one do in order to please God?" The old man replied, "Pay attention to what I tell you: whoever you may be, always have God before your eyes; whatever you do, do it according to the testimony of the holy Scriptures; in whatever place you live, do not easily leave it. Keep these three precepts and you will be saved."

Abba Anthony speaks of the God relationship and the guidance in it of the holy Scriptures (what I have called the "design"). But then he adds a precept that we are less likely to expect: "In whatever place you live, do not easily leave it." In these words I hear an admonition to dwell gladly in the present moment. It is one thing to have noble sentiments, such as compassion and concern for one's neighbor and gratitude to God, but quite another to be in the appropriate sense the *author* of these, the kind of person who through "interior strength" has etched this design upon life. Only someone self-present in the way a patient person is can practice Christian life as a *spirit* does. We must become personal focal points, definitely acting characters in God's drama. We must be focused, concentrated, consistent: Patience is a power of concentration and consistency.

Two attitudes with an outward resemblance to patience are teeth-gritting endurance and aimlessness. If we understand how these differ from patience, we will understand patience better. In the following section I shall discuss teeth-gritting endurance, but I want to set the stage with a little story.

Pookey's Umbrella

It was election night and drizzling. The hour was five fifteen and the polls were to close at six. I did not know which precinct I was to vote in and had failed in my effort to find out from a politically involved acquaintance. He thought it would probably be one of two places so I ran out the door, thinking I would take my chances and hoping to be back very soon since dinner was almost on the table.

As I rushed down the sidewalk toward the car, my four-year-old son called to me from the door that he wanted to go along. So I jogged back up the sidewalk, intending to scoop him up in my arms and be gone. But it seems that on that rainy day Pookey had discovered the joys of walking with an umbrella. He was not to be whisked in Papa's arms through the drizzle to the car; he must walk down the sidewalk, at a leisurely pace, holding his own umbrella. For this purpose, an umbrella must be sought. Mama found one after a moment or two, and Pookey walked ceremoniously down the sidewalk and across the street to the car under his umbrella, while Papa walked beside him getting a little damp, since it is more trouble than it's worth trying to walk under an umbrella held by a four-year-old. Getting into the car was complicated, since Pookey didn't want me to hold the umbrella for him but also didn't want to put it down while he got in, and of course he didn't know how to fold it like big people do. The solution he found was to get as close as he could to the open door and then jump in, abandoning the umbrella to the street. I picked it up, folded it, and slid damply into the driver's seat.

We arrived at a dilapidated concrete-block building and parked fifty feet from the door. Again I began with the assumption that I would carry Pookey quickly inside, do my business, and be gone. But again the umbrella had to be got out, and we had to walk slowly to the building. The wetness that Pookey managed to fend off with his umbrella was more than compensated for by what accrued to his feet when he walked, admiring his umbrella, through a deep puddle. When we got into the building and properly folded the umbrella, the friendly ladies sitting under the bare light bulb couldn't find my name on their list. A couple of them had ideas which precinct I belonged in, but further discussion refuted them. It was decided that I should call the courthouse. After several minutes of waiting for a clerk to find my name on the computer list, the determination of final truth was made. Pookey and I again set out into the rainy darkness, Pookey under his umbrella and I trudging along beside and above, trying to guide him around the puddles.

At the next polling place, happily, we were able to park just a few feet from the door, and there was nothing but clear sidewalk between us and it. I persuaded Pookey, more with the firmness of my voice than with rational argument, that the umbrella was not needed at this time. I voted and we headed for home. The umbrella was used one last time to get from the car to the front door of the house, where Mama met us with a cheery face and a delicious dinner.

This story narrates a situation in which patience is needed. But I have purposely omitted from the story any account of my *attitudes* toward Pookey and the delays he caused me. I do not intend to tell you what those attitudes were, but instead to explore three *possible* attitudes that a person in a situation like this might have. One of these I have called "teeth-gritting endurance," and the other two are genuine forms of patience.

In teeth-gritting endurance I feel impulses to deal abruptly with Pookey, to force him, against his will, to give up his umbrella, to disregard his concerns and regard only my own, and perhaps to become angry with him. But perhaps prudence counsels that if I behave in these ways, I will have a beastly and uncooperative child on my hands during the entire trip, which may even take the edge off the domestic bliss to which I look forward at dinnertime. I say to myself, "It isn't worth it. I shall be patient and let him have his way." And so I grit my teeth and bear with him. The reason I need to grit my teeth, as it were, is that I really do resent his coming along and causing me this delay and "unnecessary" exhaustion and inconvenience. In other words, I am quite impatient and am only suppressing impatient *behavior*, not controlling the impatience itself. Here my desires to depart from the present moment, to get away from this situation with this slow four-year-old and his dratted umbrella, are making me very *un*glad to dwell in the present moment. If I am a sufficiently good actor and have a sufficiently cool exterior—that is, if I do not *actually* grit my teeth or sigh or roll my eyes, then an observer might be misled into thinking that I am exercising patience.

Two Kinds of Patience

Patience is in contrast with teeth-gritting endurance. In real patience I am at ease with myself, dwelling gladly in the present moment despite having some desire, or what would normally be a reason to desire, to depart from it.

Before I go on to distinguish patience from aimlessness, let me use the story of Pookey to illustrate the difference between two kinds, or stages, of patience as a virtue: "practiced" and "dispositional" patience. Practiced patience is a kind that to some extent does not come naturally, and for which I therefore have to struggle. In it I may make efforts of will to be content with the present situation, not hurried or anxious, not resentful or angry. It is a form of self-control; I am working on myself to keep myself patient. It is important to distinguish this clearly from just gritting my teeth and bearing it, for what I am struggling to do is not just *endure* the situation (though unhappily) but to be *glad* in it.

I said earlier that patience is an important ground of autonomy, self-constitution, freedom. It is one of the powers by which you take an active part in shaping yourself, in being the creative author of your own character. Patience means that the individual is not at the mercy of disruptive, counterproductive, counter-moral, and unhappiness-engendering impulses and emotions and is thus also not an emotional slave to the situations that tend to make people impatient. In practiced patience, more than in dispositional, it is obvious that patience is not passivity (as the word's Latin origin suggests), but is based in activity. Patience is something you can *practice*. What might I have done, when battered that rainy election night by the impulses of impatience? There are many things, but let me mention five.

1. I might force myself to be realistic about the time scheme we were operating under. We *did*, in all probability, have time to get to the polls, and so my impatient impulses were in a sense irrational—or at least somewhat arbitrary. And dinner, though cold, would still be dinner.

2. Even if we might not make the polls by six, perhaps I could relax myself by considering how much more important it is that Pookey have a good time when he goes out with his papa than that I vote. Bringing myself to reckon realistically with the values involved in the situation here may cause that anxiety and resentment to disappear and the gladness to be dwelling in the moment, walking slowly beside Pookey in the rain, to be restored.

3. Impatience is often accompanied by muscle tension, which in turn makes one *feel* under pressure. But muscle relaxation is partly within our voluntary control. Thus simply relaxing my grip on the steering wheel, or the muscles in my stomach or jaw, can partially dispel the impulses and emotions of impatience: By relaxing my muscles, I come to see (or feel) myself differently.

4. Another technique is to go right to the center of my irritation (namely, Pookey's preoccupation with that umbrella) and find a way of looking at it that will replace such

adverse emotions as resentment and anxiety with happy ones. So I look at Pookey and his umbrella with different eyes: I see them not as a threat to my relatively trivial project of voting before six. Instead, I contemplate the beauty of Pookey's enthusiasm for the umbrella; I see him as a precious little guy glorying in the process of growing up and getting initiated into such adult things as walking with an umbrella. I envision him as a present-day Christopher Robin, with slicker and Wellingtons, dragging Pooh Bear lovingly along in one hand and umbrella in the other. Instead of focusing all my attention on what is outside the present moment—the polling place that I have yet to find, the dinner that is drying out in the oven at home—I give my attention to something beautiful right there before me. In this contemplation I become present to myself and to my son, and even though I have reasons for discontent with the present situation, I dwell in it gladly.

5. Often contemplative acts such as I have just described are fostered by physical actions and speech. For example, once we are in the dilapidated concrete-block building, a way of reinforcing my focus on the beauty of his enthusiasm for the umbrella might be to kneel down to his height, look him in the eye, and engage him in conversation about it. This not only gives him a chance to impress me with his enthusiasm, and thus to cause me to be glad to dwell in the present moment; my act of engaging him in eye contact and conversation is a physical way of focusing my attention on him rather than on the objects that are begetting my impatience.

In discussing numbers 1 through 5 above, I have described what might be called techniques for controlling and transforming the impulses and emotions of impatience. They are the kinds of response a psychologist might give if you asked, "How can I manage to be more patient with my four-year-old?" But of course people who successfully practice patience do not usually think they are employing a set of techniques for managing themselves, any more than they think of their driving skill as a set of techniques—gear shifting, braking, steering, accelerating. These *are* of course the distinct techniques by which persons control cars, but experienced drivers hardly ever think of themselves as applying such methods. They think of driving as a *single* activity. Furthermore, they hardly ever concentrate on controlling the car as such but, instead, on getting where they're going and avoiding obstacles along the way. To achieve these ends they of course apply the techniques, but they do so automatically or subconsciously. Similarly, the person who is adept at practicing patience does not normally concentrate on the techniques being used, nor even on the activity of self-control; the practice of this activity is normally quite automatic and aimed at other ends, such as the achievement of this or that goal, the reduction of personal discomfort, or (where patience is a girder of love) at the well-being of another person. It is for people who still have something to learn (and this is most of us) that it is useful to talk about these techniques, and, perhaps quite consciously, to practice them individually.

So far in this section I have tried to describe what I call "practiced patience." Practiced patience is a polymorphous skill which people can use when they are beset and attacked by emotions and impulses of impatience. But to the extent that you are successful in a given case, gladness to be dwelling in the present sets in, and there is no more need of self-control. You are at one with yourself and your immediate environment. You will remember that when I defined patience I said it was the ability to dwell gladly in the present moment when we have some desire, *or what would normally be a reason to desire*, to depart from it. In other words, for this dwelling gladly to be patience, it is not necessary that I be actively desiring to depart from it. Indeed, the more successful my efforts to overcome the desire have been, the more perfectly patient I will be.

In people who are spiritually very developed, patience may almost lose this skill-like character. Here one does not apply oneself to being patient, nor does one practice patience, even effortlessly. This kind of patience I call dispositional. Such may be, perhaps, the patience of some Christian saints. The reason such people do not need skill to be patient is that they lack the adverse impulses and emotions against which patience as a skill is directed. Their priorities in such matters as the self-esteem of a four-year-old as compared with getting to the polling place with a minimum of bother are so thoroughly correct that there is for them no question of struggling with impatience.

There is of course some reason to deny the description "patient" to a person who has no tendency toward impatience. After all, we would not normally say that a person is acting patiently if thoroughly enjoying a present activity and without any inclination to hurry it or depart from it. But we do nonetheless describe saints as patient, and for two reasons. First, a saint has achieved this state of emotional dispositions, most likely by the struggles of the practice of patience. The fact that the practice has by now entirely eradicated adverse impulses of the impatience variety leaves this psychohistorical fact standing. And, second, the situations in which we look with admiration at a saint's unstruggling and unpracticed patience are the kind that would normally give a person some reason to desire to depart from them.

Practiced patience fades into dispositional patience, or at least a momentary patience that resembles it. Because if I am thoroughly successful in overcoming my impatient impulses and emotions on election night, then I will be dwelling with thorough gladness in the present moment.

While no doubt remembering the dinner and the six o'clock deadline, I will nevertheless be entirely glad to be in the presence of my little umbrella-carrying Pookey and in consequence will have no more adverse impulses to overcome. Such a state of mind, if achieved, is a momentary snippet of sainthood. The reality, of course, is that in most cases my practice of patience is never as thoroughly successful as that; and even if, for a time, it is, I can be sure that it will not be long before I again will have need of patience-as-skill.

Patience and Aimlessness

I promised, sometime back, to distinguish patience from aimlessness. Patience has obvious usefulness to goal-oriented people. Our goals make us feel the press of time, thus making us vulnerable to impatience. The Mercedes of a typically aggressive businessman breaks down somewhere in the desert regions of Wyoming, and he finds he'll have to wait three days in a motel on the highway while a part is ordered. Here is a prime candidate for an experience of impatience. By contrast, some middle-class teenagers bumming around Europe find themselves stranded for a week by a snowstorm and experience only the mildest impulses to leave the present moment. After all, they're just drifting anyway.

The cultivation of aimlessness might seem to be a brilliant solution to the problem of impatience. We associate drifting with being happy-go-lucky. We call such people happy-go-*lucky* because they are willing to live on luck: They don't have any long-range goals, and so they take just about whatever comes along. And we call them *happy* because they are easygoing. They don't get frustrated—of course!

But apart from the mild paradox of aiming at aimlessness, there are some difficulties with this solution. First, it has practical limits: It is psychologically almost impossible to be *totally* aimless. Even the most thoroughgoing devotee of hoboism gets hungry and thus has the momentary aim of eating. But this is a trivial point when compared with another. Aiming at aimlessness, like the Stoic's project of eradicating desires, buys freedom at the price of genuine happiness. Happiness is not just the avoidance of frustration. Having some goals is an ingredient of happiness, and an ingredient of being deeply happy is having the goals proper to human life. Stoicism and aimlessness are at best coping devices, not formulas for happiness.

But even if it worked, aimlessness would not be patience. Drifters are typically not *im*patient in some of the circumstances in which goal-oriented people tend to be, but that does not mean they are patient. You will remember our definition of patience: The ability to dwell gladly in the present moment when we have some desire, or what would normally be a reason to desire, to depart from it. Drifters dwell gladly enough perhaps in the present moment, but they do not need patience to maintain their gladness in it because they have no desire to depart from it.

There is, of course, a certain similarity between aimlessness and dispositional patience, for the dispositionally patient person is precisely one who, through the practice of patience, has become trained to get clear of the impulses of impatience. And to the extent that one really is aimless, one has none of the impulses of impatience. The difference between the two is that the dispositionally patient person is one who *through the practice of patience* no longer has the impulses of impatience, who has a *training history* different from that of the aimless person. The aimless person has become trained not to have any concerns, while in the dispositionally patient person certain concerns or passions have become so dominant that the impulses of impatience which beset most people no longer exist.

Christianity contrives to make people goal-oriented. Christian character is oriented around a passion for the kingdom of God, that social order in which Christ will be gladly honored as King and his subjects will love one another as brothers and sisters, children of God. A consequence or aspect of this passion is the desire to become *fit* for the kingdom which God has promised. Speaking of a "righteousness from God that depends on faith," the apostle Paul says:

> But I press on to make it my own, because Christ Jesus has made me his own. . . . Brethren, I do not consider that I have made it my own; but one thing I do, forgetting what lies behind and straining forward to what lies ahead, I press on toward the goal for the prize of the upward call of God in Christ Jesus. (Phil. 3:12–16)

True Christians are as far from being aimless as anybody in the world, and this is one of the reasons that they need patience. If a person like the apostle did not have patience to go with the "straining forward," that person might very often be disoriented, anxious, and ineffectual.

The Fellowship of the Holy Spirit

The aim that governs the Christian's life is the kingdom of God—that situation in which God is loved with all one's heart and soul and mind and strength, and the "neighbor" as oneself. The Christian lives in this hope, and the preoccupation with it reflects itself in present dispositions toward God and neighbor. I shall begin with the love of God. How is patience a girder of the love of God? Hope, gratitude, peace, compassion for the poor and outcast, and kindness, gentleness, and forgiveness, are all shaped, as well as engendered, by the believer's standing *before*

God, walking in his *presence*. A Christian who has merely a "worldview" constructed out of the Christian concepts is in a spiritually deficient condition. No matter how strongly believing the Christian beliefs and manifesting them in behavior, that Christian lacks precisely the spiritual *vitality* of the Christian life, what is called in Scripture "the fellowship of the Holy Spirit."

There is a sense in which God is always present to everybody, indeed to everything in his creation. This is the concern of the metaphysical-theological doctrine of God's omnipresence and is quite different from the spiritual presence of God, which is fellowship with him. And just as I can control whether another human being is in my presence spiritually by paying or not paying attention to him, so I can, with practice and within some limits, control whether God is in my presence—that is, whether I am in fellowship with him—even though in another sense I cannot escape being in his presence. This aspect of control is what Brother Lawrence, a seventeenth-century Carmelite monk, called "the practice of the presence of God," and I want to explore in a moment the role of patience in this practice.

There has been a lot of loose thinking in the twentieth century about the absence of God to so-called modern "man"—as though it were somehow the fault of the age or of technology or of science when people fail to experience God's presence. Fortunately, people today talk less in this irresponsible way than they did fifteen or twenty years ago, and part of the reason for this is the renaissance of interest in the spiritual *disciplines*. It is the thesis of modern as well as ancient thinkers about spiritual formation that spiritual malformation is a result not of forces beyond our control but of a faulty spiritual *education*. It is a result of perverted habits of attention and perverted concerns. A deeply formed patience is one of the things a certain sort of modern person characteristically lacks: Superficially, such people exhibit an intense interest in getting spiritually fixed up. But they are so in the habit of being *busy* with *projects,* and in such constant and compulsive and frenetic forward and upward motion, and so oriented by considerations of cost-effectiveness and efficiency, that they have never developed powers of *contemplation*. They have not learned to dwell gladly in the present moment and thus are precluded from being friends with either people or God, for friendship is a matter of dwelling gladly in the presence of another person.

What is our attitude, for example, when Kenneth Leech tells us, in his book *True Prayer:*

> It is useful to set aside, where we can, a period of at least an hour for prayer. For St. Peter of Alcantara warns us that "if the time is too short, it is passed in unloading the imagination, and in bringing the heart under control: just at the moment when we are ready and ought to be beginning the exercise, we stop it." (P. 57)

If we are one of the "moderns" characterized above, our response will be incredulity: How could somebody have the gall to suggest that I chop a whole hour out of my busy schedule for this unproductive activity? I want to be fixed spiritually, but I want the fix to be quick; ten easy meditations of ten minutes apiece I can imagine, but an hour a day for the next thirty years? You've got to be kidding, Ken! And besides this, I know myself well enough to realize how fidgety I would become if I tried to spend a whole hour doing nothing but attending to the presence of God.

There is nothing about the modern environment as such that makes for God's absence to us, but there *is* something in modern people's spiritual education (or lack thereof) that makes for it. Patience is part of that education, and it is related to Christian fellowship with God in three ways. First, practiced patience is required in prayer and meditation, which are the primary "exercises" of God's presence. Second, practiced patience is required for allowing the spiritual exercises to do their work. And third, dispositional patience, in the context of prayer, *is* fellowship with God.

Prayer and Meditation

Prayer and meditation, though closely related, are not the same. Most prayer is conversation with God, which means both speaking to him (though not necessarily aloud) and listening to him. But perhaps we can extend the concept of prayer to include an entirely silent kind of communion as well, in which the believer simply dwells in God's presence without either speaking or listening, like two friends walking together in glad but silent awareness of their mutual presence. In this extended definition, prayer is certainly the primary form, and perhaps the only form, of communion with God. So its importance to the spiritual life cannot be overestimated.

Meditation, on the other hand, is best defined in the words of Paul as setting one's mind on the things of the Spirit (Rom. 8:5). What are some of the "things of the Spirit"? For a Christian, the most central things of the Spirit are Jesus, his life and deeds. Thus thinking about what Jesus did and said and underwent for our sakes—rehearsing his story and dwelling on various aspects of it—is primary meditation. Secondary things of the Spirit are the life and sayings of the patriarchs, the prophets and poets and sages of Israel, and the apostles and saints of the Christian church. "Meditations" that are written up for devotional use are aids to reflecting about Jesus and these other "things of the Spirit," as well as about their consequences for the living of our present life. This sort of meditation, when it is done out of spiritual hunger or when it arouses the spiritual hunger it is capable of satisfying, affects the "heart." That is, it evokes Christian emotions such as contrition, hope, joy, gratitude, compassion, and peace and other Christian states of mind such as humility and forgiveness. These states of mind are, in turn, the natural element of prayer. Contrition presses naturally to prayers of confession and petitions for forgiveness, guidance, and strength. Hope and joy lead naturally to praise and thanksgiving. Compassion and forgiveness issue in prayers of intercession for one's needy neighbor and one's enemies.

I am not saying that the order must be first meditation and then prayer. Authentic prayer can arise outside the context of any formal meditation. But even the most spontaneous prayer will have some background of reflection. After all, most people are thinking almost all the time, and it is turning their minds to the things of the Spirit which evokes such spontaneous prayer. And besides this, every prayer *contains* reflection—for example, the thought of God and what I am thankful for, in the case of a prayer of thanksgiving; the thought of God and what I am praying for, in the case of a prayer of petition; and so on.

Beginners at prayer and meditation, and sometimes even people who have been practicing them for some time, are impatient in the midst of the practice. Unlike tennis or chatting over coffee or reading a novel, this is an activity we have a hard time getting fully "into." We fidget, and feel a strong urge to get it over with, and in fact usually succeed in getting it over with in short order. If it is a morning prayer, our minds are bombarded with a dozen anxious thoughts about the day's schedule; and there we are, dwelling not in the moment of communion with God but out among the activities of the day that lies before us. If it is evening, perhaps it is nothing more than boredom or fatigue that pulls us away from prayer and meditation and toward the pillow or the Late Show.

It is not hard to see that impatience destroys prayer even more decisively than it does other activities, since a focusing of the mind is of the very essence of prayer. If you are doing woodworking impatiently, you are probably doing it badly, but at least you are still doing woodworking. But if you pray with your mind distracted by the activities that lie ahead, you are not just praying badly; you are not praying at all. For prayer is more than just sitting in a quiet place and mumbling some "prayers." It is fellowship with God, and that means dwelling in his presence. So patience is a girder of this tender, loving fellowship with God—a girder without which, because we are sinners, the entire edifice will surely collapse around us, leaving us without God in the world.

Patience in Prayer

If as praying people we are among the fidgeters, how do we practice patience in this context and thus enjoy the fellowship of the Holy Spirit more consistently? I illustrated earlier what the practice of dwelling gladly in the present moment might amount to in connection with Pookey and his umbrella. We need to approach patience in prayer with similarly concrete actions. Of course each of us is somewhat different, and it ought not to surprise us if what fits one person does not fit another, or if what is necessary for one is not needed by another. We must realize that patience in prayer is something each of us can improve in; we ought to be eager to latch onto anything that will help. Let me suggest some practices that are likely to foster patience in prayer.

1. It is important to have a comfortable position in which to pray. If kneeling is uncomfortable for you, don't do it. We are not practicing heroism in our prayer but try-

ing to fill our attention with God's glory, and if our minds are being constantly drawn to the pains in our knees, the kneeling is a (quite innocent) way of leading ourselves into temptation. On the other hand, if you do well with kneeling, by all means continue it. Just find a position that is comfortable (but not one that encourages you to go to sleep!).

2. The place of prayer has some importance. If you are surrounded by reminders of things you must do, especially things you must do soon after your prayer time is over, you are making yourself a prey to impatience. If you cannot get geographic distance between yourself and such reminders, closing your eyes during prayer is an obvious help.

3. It is good to set aside a certain *time* for prayer—both a certain part of the day and a certain duration. If it is settled in your mind that this is the time for prayer, then you become reconciled to the idea that it is not for anything else, and so you are less likely to feel quitting urges.

4. If, during the meditation part of your prayer time, a particular line of Scripture or spiritual reading touches your spirit, then just settle in and dwell on it. Because of our educational training, we are probably compulsive about finishing verses and chapters. We feel as though we ought to follow out an author's train of thought. But in spiritual reading we may resist this compulsion; our object here is to come into communion with God, and if that begins to happen during the reading, let it happen. We can think of this kind of reading as a device for listening; when, through it, we begin to hear something, the thing to do is get down to the business of listening, not keep fiddling with the device. This frame of mind in which we are *ready to hear* is something we can practice, and it is one of the practices of patience in the service of our fellowship with God.

5. There is a mental activity, called in some traditions "recollection" and among the Quakers "centering down," that is in the service of patience in prayer. In recollection you quiet down your forward urges and become present to yourself and God. You work against the dispersion of your thoughts and "center" them, "collecting" your attention on God and the things of the Spirit. Centering down is a matter of purifying your attention, collecting it all into a focal point which is the God whose identity is known through Jesus Christ. As such, centering down is the practice of the presence of God and, at the same time, the practice of patience defined as dwelling gladly in the present moment. In centered prayer the individual is "absorbed," though not in the sense of dissolved, in glad fellowship with God. But how does one go about this? I have a number of suggestions.

a. Most of us will be helped by intermingling our prayer with meditative reading. Bible-reading or the reading of some spiritual writer will help to focus our minds on God. We are, after all, focusing our minds on *God*, and the meditation will provide some thoughts in terms of which that focus can be accomplished. If we try to find fellowship with God by relying only on our own resources, we may find we draw a blank.

b. Before we start our meditational reading, it is probably good to do a kind of preliminary relaxation of our grip on the ideas and impulses that are likely to pull our minds out of the moment before God. We just sit (or kneel or whatever) quietly and try to empty our mind of the distractions that make for impatience. Silence the irrelevancies, as it were. But it is better not to do this with violence. If impulses of impatience occur at this point (as they almost certainly will), the best way to fight them is just gently to let them go. It will be counterproductive to get angry at ourselves and begin to feel like a failure. When an impulse or a distracting thought comes, just put it gently aside and slide into the interior silence once more. If it is entirely impossible to succeed in this (some days we may be just too wrought up to be able to "handle" ourselves here), then simply go on into the meditation anyway.

c. Another device for centering down is the use of some simple short prayer used repetitively. The inner silence for which we are aiming as preliminary to prayer is not a loss of conscious focus but the loss of *distracting* foci, and the concentration of the mind on the presence of God or Christ. The repetition of a simple prayer with appropriate content can help to accomplish both ends at the same time: to banish other thoughts from the mind and to concentrate the mind upon the holy one. The "Jesus prayer" from Eastern Orthodoxy can be used as such a device. It is, in its longest version, "Lord Jesus Christ, Son of God, have mercy on me, a sinner." When I am trying to center down and a distracting or impatient thought besets me, I have found that repeating this prayer with concentration on the meaning of the words is helpful in banishing it and relaxing into Jesus' presence. Another prayer that could be used this way would be the one from Isa. 6:3: "Holy, holy, holy is the LORD of hosts; the whole earth is full of his glory." If neither of these prayers fits you exactly, a little digging around should unearth one that does. What is important is that it be short and simple though rich in content, and that you get so used to using it that it comes more or less automatically as an antidote to distractions from God's presence.

d. Muscle relaxation is also an important way to resist the impulses of impatience. When your muscles are tense your whole self feels ahead of itself, ready to *go*. And of course, part of the tension is precisely due to the impulse to "go," to be gone from this activity, to be moving ahead into the future. Muscle relaxation is always within your deliberate control. Relax those muscles that feel tense, and if they tense up again, as they probably will, relax them again.

e. Concentration is aided by praying verbally, with the words even being said aloud. While earlier we saw that one form of prayer is a silent dwelling in God's presence, this is a rare kind of prayer—rare in the sense that it does not occur very often in the life of an average person of prayer, and rare in the sense that only the few people who are highly developed in their prayer life experience it regularly. If you try to dwell in a total inner silence in God's presence—unless you are very developed in prayer—it is likely that your mind will begin to wander either to those thoughts which are the impulses of impatience or to daydreaming. Or you may fall asleep! Of course it is not necessary that you be forming audible words, but your praying should probably be in sentences: utterances (even if silent) of praise, of confession, of thanksgiving, of petition. This is not to say that there should not be periods of inner silence interspersed with these "sentential" prayers, for prayer is listening as well as speaking with God. But the silences are likely to be golden opportunities for the mind to wander to other things than God. When this happens, just take up sentential praying again, and it will probably reestablish God's presence to you. Or it may be that a simple effort to banish the distracting thought or the impulse to depart from the moment will succeed. At any rate, when the utterances are concentrated heartily upon God and the silences are genuine attentiveness to his voice, then you will be dwelling gladly in the moment before God.

f. As a last word on centering down, I would report to you the wise advice of Brother Lawrence found in *The Practice of the Presence of God:*

> One way to recollect the mind easily in the time of prayer, and preserve it more in tranquillity, is not to let it wander too far at other times. You should keep it strictly in the presence of God; and being accustomed to think of Him often, you will find it easy to keep your mind calm in the time of prayer, or at least to recall it from its wanderings. (Eighth letter)

Brother Lawrence is pointing out that the centering of the mind on God is part of a pervasive *pattern* in our conscious life. Attention is in part a skill, and like any other skill, the more we practice it the more it will become second nature to us. But attention to God's presence is a very special instance of attention, connected in complicated ways with virtually the whole fabric of the Christian consciousness—with, to mention just two things, the practice of love of neighbor and the passionately felt need for what the Gospel of John calls "eternal life." If we spend our days oblivious to God's presence except for special times of prayer, it should not be surprising if those special times are rather a disappointment.

The disciplines of prayer and meditation, like most human disciplines, bear their fruit only slowly. There will be days when the entire activity seems to have been wasted, and periods when no progress is discernible. This is another reason that the Christian needs patience. It is said that Rome was not built in a day. There must have been a lot of setbacks and frustrations along the way.

We have talked about how to practice patience during the time of prayer and meditation—how to be patient in prayer in the sense that the patience itself is the dwelling contentedly in the presence of God. But what about those times when we do not succeed in prayer in this sense, when the prayer time itself is an unmitigated disaster? It is at this point that faith and hope have to be summoned in aid of patience. For even the unmitigated disaster of one day or one month's prayer time can be gladly dwelt in if we can manage to see it in the right perspective. Patience in this connection is the ability to say, with a calm heart, "I have failed; I have not filled my heart with the love of God; I have not dwelt in the temple of his Spirit as I ought to have done. But God is greater than my heart, and is faithful to his promises; and though today I fail, I know by faith that failure is not the destiny of those who persevere. And so I am glad that I have done (or am doing) the exercise, however dismal the results may look over the short haul." The practice of patience that I have described earlier is, insofar as it is successful, the dwelling in the presence of God. The practice of the patience that must make use of faith and hope is a dwelling in the absence of God, yet with a certain contentment and rest of spirit due to the consideration of God's faithfulness even in the midst of this present spiritual darkness.

Centering Down on the Neighbor

In one important way, loving one's neighbor is like praying. Prayer is not the heaping up of "empty phrases" (Matt. 6:7), even if they are very pious and orthodox ones, but involves dwelling gladly in the presence of God; and similarly neighbor-love is not just charitable actions, not even giving away all that you have to the poor (I Cor. 13:3), but involves dwelling gladly in the presence of the neighbor. Neighbor-love is to be modeled on the love of Jesus, who was Immanuel, God with us, the Holy One who dwelt patiently in our midst, ministering person-to-person to individuals. It is to be modeled on the love of the one who sat at table with outcasts and touched the sick and died among thieves, and yet is said to have experienced joy (John 15:11; Heb. 12:2) in this sacrificial identification with us. And yet despite the joy that goes with loving the neighbor, this is something for which we must struggle. Dwelling gladly in the presence of the neighbor does not often, or at first, come naturally to us, any more than does dwelling gladly in the presence of God. The neighbor is almost by Christian definition someone in whose presence it is difficult to dwell gladly. Since the neighbor can be just anyone, he or she is not likely to be someone with whom we have a lot "in common." But worse than being boring, the neighbor may be positively repulsive in one way or another or may be in some need that requires attention, time, or some kind of sacrifice. Any of these cases easily gives rise to the impulse to quit the person's presence. But besides the unloveliness of many of our "neighbors," there is the adverse effect of our own life's inertia. Our preoccupation with our own work, our own problems, our own pleasures may make the impulse to flee from the presence of the neighbor almost irresistible. And so something like centering down is needed here. I have to collect my attention upon a soul, perhaps by strategy and force, and relax the grip of impatient impulses on me, to enter into and dwell in the spiritual presence of this other human being.

But loving the neighbor is also unlike prayer in a certain way. We are not only the one called upon to love but are as often cast in the role of neighbor. We have only the vaguest notion of what it is like for God to have dealings with impatient practitioners of prayer. But we know well what it is to be the "other" in a relationship in which, through impatience, love has failed. A person with whom I once worked, and whom I desire to count as a friend, was impatient in the following way: We would be engaged in lively conversation on some topic of interest to him, and he would be vivacious and intensely involved.

Almost always this topic would bear strongly on his work, his family, his plans and opportunities. The conversation would go on for some time, after which I would turn it to a topic that bore on my interests. Precisely at this point, my colleague would look at his watch, making it evident to me that he wanted the conversation to end. This gesture of impatience, though it may seem small, became symbolic by virtue of its regularity and had a number of effects on me. At first, if I nevertheless felt it important to persevere in my topic, I would do so with a certain anxiety and a feeling of mild guilt that I was being an inconvenience. I would hurry impatiently to finish, often stumbling over my words. His impatience begot mine. After each episode I would go away tempted to feel personally devalued; being a person of fairly strong self-respect, I did not so much feel *generally* devalued as that *he* did not value me very highly. But the experience was sufficiently painful, as time went on, for me to respond by avoiding as much as I could topics that I could predict would elicit this impatient response. This meant, essentially, that there was a range of things of personal interest to me which I learned not to bore him with. Thus the relationship lacked an important dimension of mutuality. His inability or unwillingness to dwell gladly in the moment of my discoursing about my concerns limited the potential for fellowship between us. We spent lots of time together and had many interests in common and did many things for one another, and yet if he was not glad to listen when I laid my own special interests and concerns before him in conversation, I could not fully feel that he was my friend.

How does one go about centering down on one's neighbor? I have already indicated, in connection with Pookey and his umbrella, some strategies in the practice of patience, and I shall not reiterate them. Instead, I want to explore a peculiarly Christian resource of patience, a way the gospel of Christ can provide material for the practice of dwelling gladly in the presence of the neighbor. But I want to lead in to this discussion with an idea from an eminent thinker of our century, of whom a friend writes:

> In a letter . . . I spoke of the war as a "boredom," to which he replied: "I want to say something about the war being a 'boredom.' If a boy said that school was an intense boredom one might answer him that, if he only could get himself to learn what can really be learned there, he would not find it *so* boring. Now forgive me for saying that I can't help believing that an enormous lot can be learnt about human beings in this war—*if* you keep your eyes open. And the better you are at thinking, the more you'll get out of what you see. For thinking is *digestion*. If I'm writing in a preaching tone I'm just an ass! but the fact remains that if you're bored a lot it means that your mental digestion isn't what it should be. I think a good remedy for this is sometimes opening your eyes wider."

There is something in the idea of "mental digestion" for Christians to think about. The gospel of Jesus Christ provides conceptual resources for digesting experiences of all sorts, but very notably experiences of other people—of friends, enemies, and neighbors. It gives us ways of focusing on people that will keep them from being boring, irritating, and repulsive. The gospel is like stomach acid. The gospel takes experiences that the pagan mental digestive system might have to vomit up and uses them as the food of gladness. Here is part of a prayer by Mother Teresa of Calcutta, used daily by the workers in her children's home:

> Dearest Lord, may I see you today and every

> day in the person of your sick, and, whilst nursing them, minister unto you.
>
> Though you hide yourself behind the unattractive disguise of the irritable, the exacting, the unreasonable, may I still recognize you, and say: "Jesus, my patient, how sweet it is to serve you."
>
> Lord, give me this seeing faith, then my work will never be monotonous. I will ever find joy in humouring the fancies and gratifying the wishes of all poor sufferers. O beloved sick, how doubly dear you are to me, when you personify Christ; and what a privilege is mine to be allowed to tend you.

This prayer and the story that lies behind it, of God's love and his identification with sinners and sufferers and outcasts, are the acid by which Mother Teresa and her Missionaries of Charity digest experiences that would otherwise be undigestible and find in them the bread of life. Because they see the "neighbor" in terms of the story of Jesus and his love and see themselves as participants in the continuation of that story, they have a "supernatural" power to dwell joyously in the presence of persons who to the "natural" mind would be at best boring and at worst violently repugnant.

So a peculiarly Christian answer to the question of how one goes about centering down on one's neighbor is this: Remind yourself, when you are impatient, that this is a brother or sister for whom Christ died, one who, like you, is precious in the sight of God. Look at the eyes, the skin, the mouth, and listen to the voice, and remind yourself that *this* is the flesh that God took upon himself in Jesus. And so your gratitude to God is summoned up as a power of patience, and thus of love. This "contemplative" act is the Christian practice of patience as a girder of love of neighbor. When, through continued practice, this way of seeing the neighbor becomes so automatic that the practice is no longer needed, then dwelling gladly in the presence of the neighbor will have become a fixed disposition, and patience will have been swallowed up in love.

CHAPTER FOUR
PERSEVERANCE

Count it all joy, my brethren, when you meet various trials, for you know that the testing of your faith produces steadfastness. And let steadfastness have its full effect, that you may be perfect and complete, lacking in nothing.

James 1:2–4

A Virtue for Commitments

In the last chapter we explored patience, finding it the ability to dwell gladly in the present moment. Patience fits us for perseverance. If you know how to dwell gladly in the present moment, then you have won half, or more, of the battle of perseverance. Indeed, the word "patience" is often used (though more in an earlier English than now) to refer to perseverance. Patience in this sense *is* steadfastness, endurance, the ability to stick with your commitments over the long haul, or at least the ability to endure stoically to the end. But patience as I described it is not necessarily exercised in connection with long-term commitments; you can be patient with a garrulous stranger you meet on a bus, or in some short-term task like rewiring the attic or baking croissants. Perseverance, as I shall somewhat arbitrarily use the word, is related to the longer term. It is the virtue by which a person is capable, and becomes more and more capable, of keeping commitments that ought to be lifelong (or at least until death do us part). There are not many such commitments in most of our lives. Some are blessed with friendships deep and binding enough to call for perseverance; and for some there is a lifelong project, such as the eradication of racially based inequality or of cancer, which to abandon would be tantamount to taking leave of one's identity. But for most of us, the commitments in which perseverance is an ingredient are marriage and faith. And it is perseverance in connection with these two commitments which I shall discuss in the present chapter.

The New Testament word for the virtue we will look at is variously translated "endurance," "steadfastness," "patience," "perseverance." The Greek is *hypomonē*. It could also be called stick-to-itiveness. For the New Testament writers the issue is always, I think, sticking to the doctrines, life-style, and heart-orientation of the Christian faith. But we can construe this more broadly as the ability to remain true over a rather long haul to an ideal, a commitment, a person, a mission, or a job, when such remaining true is difficult because of besetting temptations, difficulties, discouragements, changes of mood, or other adversities. I am stretching New Testament usage a bit in applying perseverance to marriage; but I think we will find an examination of perseverance in marriage interesting (and maybe even helpful) both for its own sake and as a way of drawing out some of the characteristics of persevering in the faith.

When two persons marry, they make an extraordinary commitment, a promise not just to stick together until death do them part (that in itself would be bold enough) but to *love* one another that long. A friend of mine who lost her husband a couple of years ago told me that on the day he died she found a note, written probably a couple of hours earlier, in which he said simply, "Bebe, have I told you lately how much I love you?" And she said to me, "Not bad, after thirty-three years, huh?" I'm inclined to agree.

The marriage service warns about some of the bumps this love may encounter along the way: for richer, for poorer, in sickness and in health, forsaking all others. . . . But these words are only slender indicatory beams of light pricking the darkness of the future. When we commit ourselves to married love, we have only the dimmest intimations of what will threaten to break the commitment down—boredom, disappointment, inattention, work, sick children, changes in personality and interests of one or both parties—and the list could go on. The Danish thinker Søren Kierkegaard somewhere calls the marriage of children "disgusting," and I don't think it is sexual play he has in mind but the fact that marriage is incompatible with the moral makeup of the child. The ability to stick to one's commitments and tasks is an aspect of personal maturity, a dimension of what we call character or integrity. Young children are not expected to stay with anything (such as, for example, going to school) for very long unless strongly encouraged and supported by parents and teachers and social structures (in which case it is clearly not perseverance that keeps them on track). We don't take young children seriously when they make any other than the most short-term promises, because we know they are not *fit* for commitment making.

Three Aspects of Perseverance

What do children lack in lacking perseverance? One precondition of this virtue is the ability to see what one is getting into, to count the cost—and to continue vigilantly reckoning the costs as the future unfolds. This children cannot do; not having experienced enough difficulties to know what they are up against, nor made enough sustained efforts to know what inner resources are needed for bucking lassitude, fatigue, and boredom. Dark as the future is, adults who marry can have an impression of the striving this love will call for and can brace themselves to execute it. But this capacity of realistic anticipation cannot be the whole story. For there are people who stick it out with challenges of whose difficulties they had only the vaguest intimation; and others whose experience is more than enough to have equipped them with the requisite foresight, yet who seem constitutionally unable to keep their commitments.

Another precondition of perseverance is "moral passion," the appreciation of the importance of the commitment. Many people who are untrustworthy commitment makers are so not because the difficulties catch them by surprise but because they do not *care* much about the commitment. Like the ability to anticipate the difficulties, this reverence for important commitments is also an aspect of mature moral persons. They perceive the possibility of commitment breaking as a danger to the well-being of others and to their own integrity. Some children possess an analog of this appreciation, namely, a kind of compulsiveness about "duty" which is perhaps a prefiguration of moral passion. The question will come up later as to how perseverance differs from such a compulsiveness, as well as from other traits that resemble it. But let it be said for now that without vision for the beauty of faithfulness, moral perseverance is unimaginable.

But even when we have added moral passion to foresight about the difficulties, we have not yet told the whole story about perseverance. It is possible for persons to possess both of these and yet not possess perseverance. We might call such persons "weak-willed." They have enough foresight to know what they are committing themselves to, and enough moral passion to feel terribly guilty about failure to carry through with the commitment, but still they fail, and it is because of a lack of strength of will. They make efforts to keep on track, or at least would *like* to make such efforts, but fall off anyway. I think a good number of adulterers have this kind of makeup. Such persons suffer from a kind of ineptitude related to self-knowledge—self-knowledge in the sense of self-know-*how*, that is, a knowledge of how to manage temptations and how to handle the vicissitudes that beset commitments. A third element in perseverance, then, would be something like a skill of self-management in the face of commitment trials. If perseverance is indeed partly a skill, there is the hopeful prospect that it can be learned, and even that a discussion of how to meet such trials could contribute to the learning.

The Case of Thomas Davidson

In the hope of digging deeper into the nature of perseverance I invite you now to reflect with me about what seems to be an extraordinary case of this virtue, not in marriage but in a relationship instructively similar to it (and instructively different). William James records it in his memoir of his friend Thomas Davidson.

> What with Davidson's warmth of heart and sociability, I used to wonder at his never marrying. Two years before his death he told me the reason—an unhappy youthful love-affair in Scotland. Twice in later life, he said, temptation had come to him, and he had had to make his decision. When he had come to the point, he had felt each time that the tie with the dead girl was prohibitive. "When two persons have known each other as we did," he said, "neither can ever fully belong to a stranger. So it wouldn't do." "It wouldn't do, it wouldn't do!" he repeated as we lay on the hillside, in a tone so musically tender that it chimes in my ear now as I write down his confession. It can surely be no breach of confidence to publish

it—it is too creditable to the profundity of Davidson's affections. As I knew him, he was one of the purest of human beings.

We are struck with the inwardness of Davidson's perseverance: an experience of bonding, hardly at all recounted to his contemporaries, held only in memory, with a young woman decades dead. There was no present community such as Christians have, to remind and renew the commitment periodically; no sanctioning community of either law or approval, as would have existed had the woman been his living wife. Most of us find it hard enough being thoroughly faithful to our marriage commitments, even when our spouse is flesh and blood, and the law makes disentanglement ever so inconvenient, and the community adds the threat of disapproval! I remarked earlier that we can hardly call it perseverance when a child sticks to a task by virtue of a parent watching and a socialized routine that practically guarantees no escape; one of the conditions of real perseverance is that it be inwardly resourceful rather than outwardly imposed. By this standard Davidson's perseverance seems a remarkably pure specimen.

One of the theses of this book is that your relationships with others will lack maturity to the extent that you have not yet become an individual. That is, you cannot be *attached* maturely to someone else (or a community, such as the Christian fellowship) unless you are *some*body in particular, with a sort of integrity and solidity of your own. Or, put another way, you can't stand in a relationship of mature interdependence with others, as in the marriage bond or the Christian fellowship, unless you have the inward resources of a kind of independence from others. And it is my further thesis that the strength virtues—traits like self-control, patience, perseverance, and courage—

partially constitute this independence or integrity of the individual.

In our own day commitment in marriage is threatened not just by the "normal" threats to marriage, such as boredom, conflict, personality change, and so forth, but also by the calling into question of the importance and nature of the marriage commitment itself. People are saying that marriage is too restricting for genuinely liberated living, that it is passé, bourgeois, a harbor for weak and unadventurous persons. If you don't know your own mind (because in a moral sense you don't *have* a mind of your own), then you will be "impressionable." You will be as easily (and as evanescently) impressed by the ideas floating about in your social environment as the proverbial visitor to the nudist colony was by the cane-seat chairs. Or to change the metaphor, your personality will host the infection as hospitably as a body with no system for resisting alien organisms. Perseverance and courage are to the spiritual life what antibodies are to our corporeal life: a defense against disease. Marriage and Christianity seem to have this in common: that when they become unpopular it is going to take strongly *independent* people to succeed in these forms of dependency. But we can also say this: When people "succeed" in these forms of spiritual life only, or primarily, because they are popular, the "success" will only be outward and thus will not be a *spiritual* reality.

Some Doubts About Perseverance

Some doubts might reasonably arise, however, about James's moral praise of Davidson's perseverance. I hope that addressing some of these doubts will carry us to a still deeper understanding of this virtue.

James speaks of "the profundity of Davidson's affections" and seems to explain the perseverance hereby. I read him as saying that Davidson's attachment to his beloved was so all-excluding that he was nearly *unable* to enter any alternative commitment. Davidson himself says that the love with which he felt bound to the woman was such that by comparison every other woman must remain a "stranger." If this were the simple truth of Davidson's case, then perseverance would for him not be characterized, as the apostle Paul assumes it is for the Christian, as *struggle*. Other women might pursue Davidson, but they would never constitute a temptation. But would it be right to call such an unopposed passional attachment "persevering"? I think we are inclined to say no—that if a person is wholly passive in the grip of a passion, then no matter how long the passion endures, the person is not genuinely persevering in it. And in that case we are much less inclined to praise the long endurance of the attachment. However good a thing the passion may seem to us, we are inclined to write it off morally since it does not seem to be something the individual has chosen or won; it does not belong, in any deep moral sense, to the person. But Davidson's affections do not seem to have been so pure as to carry him along the path of fidelity without any help from himself, for he speaks of two temptations and says that he had to make a decision.

A closely related kind of doubt about perseverance is whether it is a virtue, after all. Is there really any difference between it and mere blindness, stubbornness, conservatism, fear of change, legalism, inability to appreciate alternatives, rigidity, and narrow-mindedness? I can imagine someone challenging Davidson: "I feel a certain irrational sympathy with the judgment that your commitment to that dead woman is heroically noble and spiritual. But what good is it, after all? You have just one life to live, and that commitment is narrowing your options and keeping you from an enriching experience of love with someone else. Why not relax the commitment—remember the girl with tender affection but become open and flexible and consider that you may not have really reckoned with what you are missing. . . . Ah! I see you do not *want* to confront that possibility. For to consider it—seriously, I mean, dwelling in all imagination on the richness you are missing—would already be to weaken your precious commitment. Like many an unhappily married person, what you call 'perseverance,' to make it sound like a virtue, is really just a sophisticated form of narrow-mindedness, a willful ignorance of the options available to you."

Perhaps we can begin to answer this challenge by remembering that perseverance is a form of *self*-mastery and thus differs from being "under" a compulsion, victimized by a fear or blindness. In his *Life of Richard Savage*, Samuel Johnson describes a person who noticeably lacked the virtue in question:

> It cannot be said, that [Richard Savage] made use of his abilities for the direction of his own conduct; an irregular and dissipated manner of life had made him the slave of every passion that happened to be excited by the presence of its object, and that slavery to his passions reciprocally produced a life irregular and dissipated. He was not master of his own motions, nor could [he] promise anything for the next day.

Notice the active language in which Johnson describes the virtue which Savage lacked: "*made use* of his abilities for the *direction* of his *own* conduct," "*master* of his own motions." And for the description of Savage's actual state of character he uses passive language: "the *slave* of every passion that *happened* to be *excited* by the presence of its *object*." A person who kept on the track of commitments out of an overpowering fear of change or mere lassitude and dislike for new experiences, or a person who did not venture out of old commitments for lack of imagination and appreciation of the opportunities that were waiting, would not be persevering. Steadfast persons are those who direct their own lives and therefore have sufficient insight into what they are doing and who they are and what their options are to be able to choose intelligently.

But even if Davidson is not a victim in his perseverance, there remains the question: "What good is it, after all?" Why persevere in a commitment that has its disadvantages, to put it mildly? By utilitarian standards, perseverance or not, Davidson has made an almost certainly erroneous decision. For he has cut himself off from the possibility of marital happiness for the sake of—what? A bittersweet memory? A sense of commitment and his own integrity?

Davidson's perseverance is at the opposite extreme from Savage's "irregularity," and I think that the contrast between the two men may be instructive for answering the question, What good is perseverance to the person who possesses it? Johnson twice calls Savage "dissipated," suggesting not only that he is a slave of his passions and circumstances but also that he has no inner *center*. His soul is scattered abroad, or at least is very easily scatterable by the winds of context; he has no weight, no solidity, no integrity. For what is integrity? It is the ability to hang together, to remain an entirety, to be something in particular and to remain that something despite the pushing and pulling of the environment. It is to be what Kierkegaard calls a "single individual."

Someone once wrote of the composer Felix Mendelssohn that he was "like a man who is only jolly when the people he is with are all jolly anyway, or like one who is only good when he is surrounded by good men; he does not have the integrity of a tree which stands firmly in its place whatever may be going on around it." To say that a person is "flexible" or "adaptable" or "other-directed" in this way is a moral reproach. Mendelssohn is not as *obviously* "dissipated" as Savage; he was not socially offensive in the ways Savage was. If he was indeed dissipated, it is to the credit of a person's moral and psychological judgment to be capable of noticing this fact. Though Mendelssohn was hardly the social menace that Savage was, he no less lacked a "self."

But Davidson, it seems, had one. And this would be one way to justify James's praise of Davidson's perseverance. When he speaks of the "profundity of Davidson's affections," perhaps he is not speaking just about their "intensity" but about the fact that when Davidson had an affection, it was really *his*. It belonged to Davidson because there was a self there, one with historical continuity, which made having an affection something morally significant.

Perseverance is an activity or process (earlier I called it the exercise of a self-management skill) by which one *consolidates* oneself. In the *practice* of perseverance in a context like marriage, the self is formed by acquiring an interior history or continuity. A person who does not actively form a moral identity which endures through time is necessarily dissipated. To focus exclusively, or even primarily, on richness of experience and opportunities for enjoyment and fulfillment, as our challenger of Davidson's perseverance did, is to wade in the shallows of hedonism and to ignore the deeper waters of the human self.

Memory and Persevering Love

Let us now leave the airy example of Davidson, who never had a squabble with his lover in the last thirty years of their relationship, and turn to the joys and difficulties of persevering in love to a spouse who is present in body and mind. What is it to persevere in your promise to love until death do you part when, after three weeks of love together, the excitement of conquest fades and a certain lassitude begins to supervene upon the wish fulfilled? How do you remain steadfast in your love when, after a couple of years of marriage, a colleague at the office is just plain more exciting, more interesting, more fun to be with than your spouse? What is it to keep the marriage vows at five o'clock on a Friday afternoon, when the older child is terrorizing the younger, and it has been going on like that for the last two hours, and your spouse is about to break into tears, and you are dog-tired from whatever it is you have been doing all day, and you step into the bedlam with a strong inclination to duck, and she greets you at the door with "You take over; I've had it!"? What is it to be faithful when the children, who have been shockingly central to your bond for the past twenty-two years, have all gone off to college and you look across the breakfast table at a bald pate glimmering behind the newspaper in the morning sunlight, and it dawns on you that there's nothing you want to *say* to him?

So: The last of the children has left for college, and there you sit in the silence, a bowl of bran flakes with raisins before you, and behind that the vase of rosebuds you picked in the garden this morning, and behind that another bowl of bran flakes, and then the newspaper with the shiny globe behind it, on which the morning sunlight dances. You haven't seen any eyes for several minutes, and besides that you're not eager to. But your lack of eagerness—the fact that it doesn't even make you angry that he is so uncommunicative—*does* bother you. What is becoming of this marriage (let's not be so pessimistic as to ask, "What has become . . .")? Something has slipped, though, you hope, not beyond retrieval. How can you persevere in love to this man, in this moment when the love between you has fallen into a deep sleep?

You could, of course, impulsively and a little self-righteously say, "Henry, put that newspaper down right now and *talk* to me!" Now, you know him better than I do, but my hunch is that that's not the best strategy if your purpose is to awaken the love and not just Henry. Eventually he will need to be drawn into communion, but perhaps it will be better if you prepare yourself a bit by waking up your own love for him. One technique I want to suggest is a certain use of *memory*. I'll bet you've had some wonderful times together. Remember the summer you worked so hard, side by side, renovating that lakeside cabin that the previous owners had let go almost to ruin? (Some of the most precious moments that summer were the coffee breaks, midmorning and midafternoon, when you took your ease and contemplated with common pride the work you'd done.) Or that motor trip across a hot Quebec when you were courting. Why would anyone drive across Quebec in July? you asked yourselves after you'd done it, but you agreed together that it had been a wonderful time. Or the birth of your first baby. Henry was so endearingly childlike in his excitement about that prunelike little red anthropoid, and so solicitous about the delicate condition of the new mother.

The exercise I suggest is this. Take a memory that endears Henry to you, a memory of happy common life or of some special affection shown you, and use it as a grid through which to contemplate that aging person across the table. See him through the eyes of pleasant memory. Do not *do* anything yet, or *say* anything, but just take some time to look at your partner in this complimentary light. If you can't think of anything complimentary—if your hostility or indifference has grown to that point—try a little harder. Perseverance is not easy. You may have to shed some grudges (as Christians say, "die to yourself") just to admit to yourself that this is the person of whom those happy memories are memories. But if you succeed in seeing him this way, you will find that some affection will come over you. You will love Henry because he will *look* more lovable to you. Then, when you find your heart enlivened toward him, your behavior will naturally become more affectionate, and in the interaction that ensues perhaps you can gently remind him of some of the pleasant memories that have reawakened your love, and so reinforce the response that your expressed affection will naturally beget. I think you will find that when you explicitly share with each other the happy memories of your past love, those memories will have an even stronger tendency to arouse present affection in you both.

This technique for persevering in love is just the reversal of what happens in grudge bearing. The grudge bearer also dwells on memories of a relationship with another person and sees the other through the grid of those memories. But instead of dwelling on happy experiences and scenes from their past which are complimentary to the other person, he or she dwells on offenses (many imaginary, no doubt). Thus the grudge bearer descends into a confirmed disposition of seeing the other in an uncomplimentary light, which we call hostility. Hostility, in turn, disposes the grudge bearer to see only uncomplimentary things in the other and also, of course, tends to evoke unpleasant behavior which reinforces the uncomplimentary light in which the other is seen. When we become aware of the dynamic of grudge bearing, we can turn it to the service of love by *practicing* the contemplation of happy memories of our relationship and of praiseworthy actions of our partner. When this practice has become an ingrained habit and skill of self-management, then we have one of the powers of perseverance in marriage.

The Memory of God's Faithfulness

Our affection for God and his kingdom is as subject to temporary dullness as affection for our spouse; and like the latter, if we do not persevere, the dullness can gradually overtake and drown us altogether. In marriage, this drowning is the moral equivalent of divorce; in our God relationship, of "falling away" or apostasy. It is worth noting that just as a couple can be spiritually divorced while living together, having a passable sex life, and remaining "faithful" to each other, so a person can be a spiritual apostate while remaining a contributing member of the church and creedally impeccable. The substance of faith is joy and peace and hope in the gospel, just as the substance of marriage is heartfelt tenderness and affection for your spouse; so it is these, and not just toeing the behavioral line, that perseverance aims to preserve.

Most of us can remember times when God lifted us out of the pit of despair, or gave us the comfort of his mercy when we were rejected by those around us, or flooded us with the presence of his Spirit in a time of doubt. In memory we can return to these past moments of glory as anchors and points of departure for pressing forward. There is a spiritual skill to be learned here, a habit of drawing on what is best in our past God relationship for resources with which to meet the future. We must exercise good judgment about which among those moments are worth drawing on for present inspiration. And no doubt as we mature, we will see significance in some of our past moments that meant little to us earlier, and we will come to have less regard than formerly for moments that we once cherished. This is all a part of spiritual growth and of growth in the Christian virtue of perseverance.

There are misuses of memory. A stereotype revivalist hearkens back sentimentally to the moment when he was "saved." The story is told and retold, and in a sense the memory becomes the anchor point for the revivalist's present religious life and infuses it with a certain vitality and maybe steadiness. But real perseverance may be missing here, for the revivalist seems not just to take *encouragement* from the memory but to *live* in it. His religious life not only had its beginning in that moment of conversion but also, it seems, its *end*. Perseverance can make use of happy memories of the God relationship, but there is also a forgetful element in it, expressed by the apostle Paul when he said, "Forgetting what lies behind and straining forward to what lies ahead, I press on toward the goal for the prize of the upward call of God in Christ Jesus" (Phil. 3:13–14).

Paul also said that "whatever was written in former days was written for our instruction, that by steadfastness and by the encouragement of the scriptures we might have hope" (Rom. 15:4). He seems to refer to the fact that the "memory" that can happen when we meditate on the Scriptures can "encourage" us—that is, renew our hearts—when we have become disheartened and dulled; and in doing so it contributes to our establishment in the faith. We have an explicit example of this strategy in chapters 11 and 12 of the book of Hebrews. In chapter 11 the author rehearses the Bible's witness to the faithfulness of God and the faith of many men and women of God. And then he says:

> Therefore, since we are surrounded by so great a cloud of witnesses, let us also lay aside every weight, and sin which clings so closely, and let us run with perseverance the race that is set before us, looking to Jesus the pioneer and perfecter of our faith, who for the joy that was set before him endured the cross, despising the shame, and is seated at the right hand of the throne of God.

> Consider him who endured from sinners
> such hostility against himself, so that you may
> not grow weary or fainthearted. (Heb. 12:1–3)

In the midst of calling the Hebrews to take courage from the faith of their forebears, the author recalls to them also the faithfulness of Jesus who is not only, as the incarnate Son of the Creator, the *perfecter* of their faith but also the *pioneer*, who, like us, had a human race set before him to run. He is an encouragement to us because he ran it to the end with courage and joy. The author of Hebrews seems to be writing to people who are fighting not only against inward dullness but also against outward pressure to give up their faith. But even if we are not being persecuted, it seems clear that "remembering" people who lived by faith can encourage us in times when the Christian heart seems to have gone out of us.

The preacher who lays before the congregation stories of faithful ones is not just providing models or guiding the congregation but is also encouraging it. The story may be Abraham's or Sarah's or Joseph's or Moses' or Amos' or Jesus'; or it may be that of Francis of Assisi or of Søren Kierkegaard or Dietrich Bonhoeffer or Edith Barfoot or Thomas Merton or Mother Teresa of Calcutta or Dorothy Day. But one of the effects of recalling that "cloud of witnesses" one by one—their courage, their hope, their weaknesses, their joy and thankfulness, their sins, their stalwart resistance to the forces of hatred—is that this remembrance *renews* us. It is as though these stories, vividly and passionately told, say to us in our discouragement: "Yes, it can be done; yes, there is a faithful God whose Son is Jesus; yes, ordinary sinners can grow into saints after all; yes, the life lived in obedience before God is a thing of beauty, a pearl indeed." These stories have the power to put our dullness into a certain perspective, and thus to weaken its grip, and so when we hear them with our hearts, a bit of perseverance has been induced in us. But we should not rely passively on our preachers to induce this perseverance. Each of us should learn some stories (or maybe just one) that especially touch us, which can become a kind of light for us in times of spiritual darkness.

Marriage as Work and Fun

You've been married to her for three weeks now. It was no easy matter convincing her to settle down, and the sense of accomplishment has been enormous—having such a pretty, bright young woman as your *very own wife!* Such a credit to you in the eyes of your friends, and comfort after the long loneliness of your bachelorhood. Not to speak of all the delicious snuggling, and so forth. But in the last day or two a gray mist of satiety and realism has begun to envelop and darken the joys. Not that you're panicking—yet. But you have sensed faintly, in the recesses of your mind, ominous potentialities. The anxiety has made you irritable, and a couple of times there has been some bad energy between you. And this of course arouses further anxieties. It seems that the time has come to begin the exercise of perseverance.

It is not that you were unaware that marriage is "hard work." The philistines have been saying this as long as you can remember, and in your own way you have owned it, seeing it vividly in a couple of marriages you're privy to. But now it begins to bear seriously in on you that marriage is a *task*, full, like many tasks, of joys for the one who undertakes it, but nevertheless a challenge calling for self-denial and effort. You begin to see the truth from the inside, to feel the weight of it bearing down upon your head and shoulders. When she gets defensive about her mother, you need to check your inclination to needle her further and instead maybe find something good to say about the old dear. When she takes for granted (and reminds you) that a husband ought to serve his wife tea in bed, maybe you should swallow your hurry and your pride and go get the tea. (And swallow too the impulse to set it down sullenly and go on your way; give her a lingering kiss with it.)

Oddly enough, perceiving the marriage as a task is a dawning comfort. The visceral admission that married love is an ethical challenge and not merely an aesthetic delight quiets the anxieties, brings on a certain patience with your own and your lover's lapses, and lifts, a bit, the cloud that was beginning to darken the joys. Seeing that marriage is work liberates you to experience it as fun. Seeing it as an arena of moral activity, not just as a blessing conferred (or conquered) for the purpose of security and satisfaction, renders it capable of being a satisfaction and security.

So we have here another of the resources of perseverance. It consists in acknowledging and aggressively holding before my mind that love is something I must win in deepening my personality through sacrifice. There is a passive conception of married love abroad these days. One hears people say, "After a while, we just didn't seem to have anything in common." As though having enough in common to sustain a marriage is something that just drops down from heaven. Or we are like Bertrand Russell, who tells us in his autobiography,

> I went out bicycling one afternoon, and suddenly, as I was riding along a country road, I realized that I no longer loved Alys. I had had no idea until this moment that my love for her was even lessening.

As though love is beyond the reach of our responsibility, either gripping us or not, and that's the end of it. People see themselves as pawns in the hands of love; it is like the wind, which "blows where it wills, and you hear the sound of it, but you do not know whence it comes or whither it goes." We are all to some extent in the grip of this picture of love, and so its takes some reminding and some efforts to see things otherwise. But when we do learn to see love as our responsibility, we have learned one of the resources of perseverance in marriage. So this virtue is in part the disposition to remind ourselves, in appropriate moments, that marriage is not so much a haven as an open sea, not so much a prize as a contest in which the object is to win ourselves in love for our partner.

Faith as Warfare and Blessing

In the New Testament, faith is often pictured as an athletic contest, a "good fight," as finding the narrow gate. Indeed, one test by which you can help determine whether your "faith" is *Christian* faith is the question: "Does it require perseverance?" If the answer is that it has become quite smooth sailing for you, then either you are a very highly developed saint or your notion of faith has become insipid.

> Abba Poemen said of Abba John the Dwarf that he had prayed God to take his passions away from him so that he might become free from care. He went and told an old man this: "I find myself in peace, without an enemy," he said. The old man said to him, "Go, beseech God to stir up warfare so that you may regain the affliction and humility that you used to have, for it is by warfare that the soul makes progress." So he besought God and when warfare came, he no longer prayed that it might be taken away, but said, "Lord, give me strength for the fight."

The "warfare" may be the struggle with intellectual

doubts; or the overt fight against disease and hunger and racism and exploitation of the weak by the powerful; or an inner contest with lust, greed, indifference to the poor and afflicted, laziness in prayer, or your attitude toward someone the sight of whom galls you; or it may be the rejection and humiliation you suffer for your witness to Jesus. As Abba John the Dwarf learned from the old man, if nothing of this sort constitutes an "enemy" for you, you should probably take a second look at your "faith" and pray God to call your enemies out of the bushes.

In some ways marriage and faith are unnatural to the human spirit, so we must be trained in them, *bent into shape* for them and by them. If we are naive about this (and most of us are), we will quite predictably be weak. When the difficulties come we will either avoid them, by compromising the intensity of our partnership or the authenticity of our faith, or be dismayed like an army caught in a surprise attack. Vigilance about dangers, an honest reckoning with the difficulties, "counting the cost," is thus an essential feature of perseverance.

How does the Christian cultivate this watchfulness? One natural way is to alternate between anticipatory reflection in quiet and acts of courageous acknowledgment in the midst of temptations and challenges. In your morning prayer you acknowledge before God that temptations to unfaithfulness are real and will most certainly come your way today. In imagination you rehearse some for the sake of vividness. This anticipatory meditation puts you on alert for difficulties. Then when you are called upon to speak gently the word of truth concerning racism in the company of racists, or to act in compassion toward someone who fills your worse nature with scorn, you reduplicate the quiet resolve by acknowledging in the concrete circumstance that the time for self-denial has arrived; the time for action consistent with your deep commitments is *now*.

A related strategy of perseverance is that of putting the obstacles that make perseverance necessary into their spiritual-pedagogical context. Perseverance is not just a faltering corrective for the damnable condition that the world and our souls are in; it is selfhood, maturity, the strength for which the child of God is destined. "Count it all joy, . . . when you meet various trials, for you know that the testing of your faith produces steadfastness. And let steadfastness have its full effect, that you may be perfect and complete, lacking in nothing." So the apostle James. The same theme is struck in Hebrews 12, Romans 5, and elsewhere. This psychological truth about the effect of suffering and temptation triumphed over is also an encouragement, one which the biblical writers did not neglect to employ and which all Christians would well ponder in their hearts and appropriate to their self-understanding.

Perseverance and Time Awareness: I

Your son is four and your daughter is two. A third child is expected in November. It is a Friday late in July, and you have been working hard all day on a book due in early September. The workday is over and you have arrived at your door, having walked home a couple of miles across town in the afternoon heat. Stepping inside, you are greeted by screams—not the delighted squeals of "Hi, Papa" that often restore your spirit, but howls of distress from one voice and of recrimination from another. You have come upon a scene of terrorist activities, and your daughter is not the only victim (or perhaps the primary intended victim). Your wife is almost in tears. Neither child took a nap, and the pressure has been constant; she appears to be almost as drained as you are and, like you, wants nothing but relief at this point. What does it mean, right now, to persevere in your commitment to love this woman till death do you part?

Or: At the factory there is a colleague of yours, another accountant, on whom you find yourself expending more and more attention. At coffee breaks and lunch you gravitate naturally together; you are never at a loss for something cute to say to each other. He leaves silly notes in your box, and you have taken to reciprocating. By comparison your husband seems humdrum; your conversation with him is never as light, vivacious, and free as it is with your colleague. If the question were put, you think you could say you still love your husband, at least residually; but the slope you are on with your friend is slippery and increasingly steep. If you let yourselves go, it is just a matter of time before this thing gets out of hand. How do you persevere in your commitment to love your husband until death do you part?

The scenes I have just described are moments of adversity in the life of married love, occasions calling for the exercise of perseverance. To any such moment we bring an implicit sense of our location in time, and how we focus that sense and exploit its elements is another aspect of perseverance. I have already mentioned the use of memory in perseverance, so I will now focus on our sense of the future. At the beginning of this chapter I said perseverance is a virtue that equips us for the long haul, and it is precisely the connection between the sense of belonging within the long haul and the urgency for present activity that is so essential to genuine perseverance. The persevering person lives neither in an abstract present (thus living from "moment to moment") nor in an abstract future (perhaps as in the popular picture of the "stoic" whose goal is just to "hold out" till the end) but in a present informed by the future, conceiving it as something that must be lived unto in the responsible acts of the present. That person knows commitment is possibly for a very long time but mutes its potential grandiosity by focusing on loving faithfulness in the present moment.

While knowing that love is something always to be practiced in the here and now, the one who perseveres invests the here and now with a singular significance by construing it as belonging to the long haul and being, in a sense, in the service of the long haul.

On that Friday afternoon when you return home and stick your head into the bedlam, your first inclination is to duck back out the door. Since that's not possible, your second impulse is to curse or plead fatigue and abdicate responsibility or, at a minimum, to sulk as you act "responsibly"—that is, to join the children and let your wife be the grown-up in the situation. To put it mildly, this is not the loving course of spirit. So this is what you will have to fight.

The childish response expresses an emotional habit we might call "love-atomism," the disposition to conceive love as more or less *episodic*. According to love-atomism, we love when we feel good about each other and cease to love when we do not. Married love-atomists may be lucky enough to feel good, most of the time, about their spouses, so such love may even endure for quite a while. But it does not have the persevering attitude characteristic of married love, and given the adversities that love runs into, love-atomism is a weak foundation for long-term relationships such as marriage and mature friendship. In marriage we need an antidote for love-atomism, and the most essential antidote is training our minds on the long haul. When you are inclined to duck out the door or begin sulkily to set the table and wash the children's hands, you need to "die to yourself" and act affectionately and magnanimously and responsibly instead. And I am suggesting that a resource for accomplishing such acts of will is that of attending to the long-term *significance* of those needed acts, namely, that the moment in which you are called upon to perform them is a time segment in the larger project of married love. If you form in yourself the habit of seeing the cheerful setting of the table and the patient washing of the children's hands as contributions to that larger commitment, then you will have turned the tables on the love-atomist in yourself and learned some deep perseverance.

You would have to be an extremely naive married person not to know that your single actions have the significance of contributing to or frustrating the long-term project of married love; but I think it is quite common for a person not to *attend* to this significance, to *practice* the awareness of it. And when we do not, though we may be ideologically committed to marriage, we are at least partially, from the point of view of our consciousness, love-atomists. If hugging your wife despite your inclination to flee or sulk or let some angry words fly vindictively at her were not a part of that vista of till death do you part, then you would surely not hug her. You would rather go with the impulse-atom of the moment. I am suggesting that you take this ordinary psychological fact and turn it to the advantage of perseverance by holding that vista quite self-consciously before your mind. It will give you a certain distance from the sufferings and impulses of the moment and invest your loving actions with a significance that emerges as a motive.

Perseverance and Time Awareness: II

In the case just described, contemplation of the commitment comes to the aid of loving in the moment of present adversity. But there are times when the adversity comes more from the side of the commitment, the terror of the long haul, the sense that you will never make it that long. You feel swamped in the *enormity* of the commitment to love until death do you part.

Though you are bound by marriage to your husband, your colleague with the flashing smile and the lively practical jokes has all the present attention of your heart. Your idea of marriage is traditional, and so involves for you the commitment to your husband "as long as you both shall live" rather than, as in the modern version, "as long as you both shall love." That is, for you it is the commitment that holds up the feelings, not the feelings that support the "commitment." Which is to say, the virtue of perseverance has a use in your married life. But you are in a panic, precisely *because of this commitment*. Can you hold out? You begin to have dreams about your husband dying. And then about yourself dying.

It is a piece of peasant wisdom that when you are struggling with yourself for a distant goal or the long term, an important way to fend off discouragement is to take bite-size chunks of the task. The advice of Alcoholics Anonymous is "one day at a time." The alcoholic knows, certainly, that the goal is to stay on the wagon indefinitely—that is, until death. But the prospect of indefinite abstention is so daunting to one with the alcoholic's compulsion that to dwell on the long term is to court disaster. And so the alcoholic learns to focus (and the meetings are designed to help the focus) on the task of abstaining for the next twenty-four hours. If the alcoholic can abstain that long, and do this every day for life, he or she will have persevered indeed!

The same is true of marriage. If you are having difficulties, the prospect of loving this man for the next thirty or forty years may overwhelm and discourage. But what about loving him for the next twenty minutes? Why not try filing the long haul in the back of your mind and hugging him right now and trying, just for the next ten minutes, to hear what he has to say, not just with your ears but with your heart? Doing so may give you an emotional lever on your colleague's attractions when you see him at the office tomorrow. Listening with your heart for those ten minutes may open your husband's face to you and blot some of the humdrum out of your impression of him. Not to mention the fact that it may liven *him* up and bring out something endearing in him that has lately got blanketed over in dullness.

Then, at the office tomorrow, don't think to yourself, "I know I won't be able to hold out against this person's charms forever." Instead (with the "forever" no doubt in the back of your mind), do something decisive against his charms *this morning*. Abstain, just for now, from that little note-in-the-box routine that's been getting you gripped by him. Then, when you're chatting with him over coffee, turn the conversation to something that your husband has done or said, giving the message of your husband's importance to you. You can think of a dozen other things you can do, just for the moment, by way of detaching yourself. Acts like these will be painful, no doubt. If the enormity of your commitment panics you, the technique of "one day at a time" may relax you just enough so that you can do some things that need doing if you are to make good on that commitment.

Faith: The Promise and Today

When one marries one enters into a covenant that stands as an objective context in which the two individuals now find themselves, for better or for worse. But the covenant to love till death do us part can never be carried out otherwise than in the today of the relationship. The fact of the covenant gives orientation, a sense of something tied down, resolved, something that does not need to be questioned, reestablished, raised again as an issue. It is a source of security for love, a frame in which it can be acted out with minimal anxiety. But the fact that nothing more is ever concretely required of a person, in the keeping of this covenant, than keeping it today has also a certain comfort in it. I have tried to show, in the preceding two sections, how these two facts about marriage may be capitalized on for perseverance, and how this virtue is in part the skill of knowing when and how to focus attention on one or the other of these facts as particular marital difficulties arise.

Christian faith has parallel dimensions. Faith is the trait of believing that, in Jesus of Nazareth, God has reconciled sinners to himself and promised membership in an eternal kingdom of righteousness; and in expectation of that kingdom and longing for it, of reflecting, in some small way at least, the character of what will one day be fully in force. The objective context in which Christians believe themselves to stand is that sovereign act by which God has reconciled a sinful world to himself. But faith is not just belief in that context, any more than marriage is just the acknowledgment of its covenant. Without the dimension of "today"—the today in which the anticipation of God's kingdom is played out in love of neighbor and of God, in joy and hope and patience, in gratitude and self-control and compassion, in gentleness and mercy and forgiveness and holiness—no disposition would be Christian faith.

Like marriage, faith inevitably encounters rough sledding, which calls for perseverance. For five years or so, my wife and I did "Christian work" in an economically deprived community on the edge of the city in which we lived. We preached the gospel amid flying spitballs and children making sudden dashes for the rest room, taught in and ran a raggle-taggle Sunday school, tried to attend to some of the physical and emotional needs of the people, and organized church picnics, trips to a local farm, and other social fare. Our tenure there was brought to a face-saving end by events that carried us away for a year to the bliss of a community nestled between some lakes in rural Minnesota.

But long before we left, my enthusiasm for this ministry had begun to dull. I longed for an audience who would *listen*, who would take sufficient interest in the Word of God that it might begin to get under their skin, who could understand words like "faith" and "sin" in just a tiny bit more than the simplistic way these folks did. I longed to see some response to our ministry, just one slightly improved life, for example. And of course there were less noble reasons for wanting a change.

Lots of Christian work is like the work we did there, and it doesn't have to be in the slums to have these qualities: not interesting in any immediate way, high in investment of energy and low in dividends of transformed lives. Sometimes you engender enormous activity, but the discouragement is that it can all seem so meaningless. And so there is the nagging urge to quit, and your continuation in the work, if you do continue, is not so much perseverance as a kind of inertia, an inability to say no, a fear of the embarrassment that quitting would entail. I don't deny that some Christian "ministries" are in fact meaningless, nor that there come times when you should brush the clinging dust of a ministry from your feet and go on down God's road. But there are also times to persevere, and our present inquiry is how that is done.

As I look back on the work I have just described, I see much faithlessness in it. It was not just an ineffectual ministry—that in itself would not be faithlessness—but to a great extent a lapse in love and obedience to God. Though I showed up Sunday after Sunday, and other days of the week as well, I was for the most part not exercising the virtue of perseverance; and the evidence is that I didn't take much *joy* in the work. I often lacked that larger perspective which enlightens the work of the present moment. And that larger perspective is of course that God has encompassed even the less advantaged places of this world, with their trash, odd smells, rough language and behavior of both children and adults, illiteracy and indifference to what I have to say—in Jesus, God has hugged the human beings of that setting to himself and said, "They belong to me and are precious in my sight." When at the climax of my sermonette Huck Finn lobbed the world's largest spitball and hit the pianist in the ear, wrenching away the eternal moment I was about to create and reducing the entire scene to slapstick, real perseverance would have been this: To remember that Huck and all those other laughers in the congregation are God's beloved children, the very individuals out of whom he will one day constitute his promised kingdom. To have the toughness of spirit to hold to that vision and its attendant love even in the midst of the utter failure to get anyone to pay attention to it, because you know that in God's sovereign love he *will* see that it is realized—that is perseverance.

Just as in marriage, so in faith: tapping the larger perspective to invest the present moment with new (or old) significance is often what is needed to persevere in love. But also, as in marriage, so in faith: If you begin to lose your grip on the larger perspective, a tactic for regaining it is to hunker down with a vengeance into the present moment and quite self-consciously act out the significance of that larger perspective. If your faith in God's kingdom and its coming is growing hazy, go visit that lonely old man who lives in the hut on the ridge, and do it quite consciously as imitation of the compassion with which God, Immanuel, visited us in our abandonment and need. Or if your hostility toward the spitballer for what he did to your moment of eternity makes it next to impossible to see him as a child of the kingdom, then make it a point, after the service, to give him a hug (just as God has done in Jesus), or go around, middle of the week, and take him out for an ice-cream cone. Such acts of following tend to enliven our vision of the whole and get us back on the track of seeing the world aright.

Conclusion

This book has been about the nature and practice of "the virtues of willpower." One who possesses these is in possession of *himself*, or *herself*, not "the slave of every passion that happen[s] to be excited by the presence of its object." And if for strength each of us draws also on the grace of God in Jesus Christ and on the promise of the perfect fellowship of heaven, then the spiritual strengths are the strengths of a Christian. By way of conclusion, let me add two or three comments.

My language has perhaps on occasion sounded moralistic. In our age "moralistic" is a term of abuse. We don't think professional people should "moralize" or cast themselves in the role of "moralists." To be a moralist is to be a busybody, not a noble soul and a blessing to humankind, as was once thought. The truth, of course, is that anybody who thinks at all about human concerns ends up moralizing in some sense, even if the moral is only that moralizing is a very bad and narrow-minded thing, and that nobody should be a busybody. A friend of mine recently declared the psychologist Albert Ellis to be on the lunatic fringe because he exhorts his patients to be *reasonable!* (Not because he might have a superficial conception of what it is to be reasonable.) Such is the spirit of our age. If in the clinic you bare your values even so much as to endorse reasonableness, you qualify for membership in the fringe.

I have tried here to challenge both you and myself. The life of love, and the power to love that we may come into possession of, is something for which each of us has responsibility, to which each of us can and should be challenged. If we lack self-control, patience, and perseverance, it is because we have not practiced these things. It is a failure for which we can be called to account, whatever may be the environmental factors that encourage it.

The moralizing tone you may have heard is no typographical error. A book about these virtues which was not "moralizing" would by that fact be framed in a setting foreign to them. Like seeing a lion in a twenty-by-thirty-foot zoo cage. In a sense you are seeing a lion, all right. But what a false impression you get unless you see the animal in its natural habitat, roaming, hunting, keeping the lionesses in line. Most of the "ethics" by philosophers and theologians is like that: In a sense it is about the issues of ethics, but its rhetoric is unfitting, so it gives a false impression of the thing it is supposed to make clear. My conviction is that ethics—even philosophical and theological ethics—ought to be presented in as natural a habitat as possible; and when a description of the virtues is cast in *that* rhetoric, the tone of challenge is inevitable.

But if you are a very modern person, moralizing might offend you not just because it challenges you. You might not mind being challenged to be sincere or authentic, to "find yourself" or to "get in touch with your feelings," or to assert yourself and look out for number one. But the challenge here is to the old-fashioned stuff about loving one another; and behind the assumption that this takes self-control, patience, and perseverance is the further supposition that love requires sacrifice, self-opposition, dying to yourself.

Most of us have what I would call the "grunt conception" of efforts of will. To try to love somebody or overcome your fear of something or be patient with a senile person or persevere in your marriage are, according to the grunt conception, primitive acts of a faculty we supposedly all have in us called "the will." And just as you can flex the biceps on your right arm just by *doing* it (that is, "at will"), so you can exercise your will just by doing it (that is, you can will at will!). If you want to love somebody but don't feel like it, then you just grunt inwardly, and if you fail it's because you didn't try hard enough. Where this crude and unrealistic conception of will is in operation, it is no wonder that moralizing has received a bad name.

This book has been, in its own way, an onslaught on the grunt conception of willpower, and so it has been an attack on moralizing. Willpower is not a matter of blind spiritual effort, of grunting oneself to sainthood, but of practical wisdom, *finesse* in the management of one's impulses and emotions and moods. To have the virtues of willpower is largely a matter of knowing yourself and knowing how to get around yourself, of knowing how to take strategic advantage of dispositions and powers that are already within you. In the case of love, it is the use of memory, of imagination, and the power of conception to tease out of yourself what inclinations to love are already there; to take advantage of stimuli in your environment and habits already present within you to nurture what is good in yourself and root out what is evil.

Though every Christian has the Christian resources of self-mastery more or less available, each person has these and other resources in more or less idiosyncratic ways. What works for one person may not work for another; each must hew an individual path toward inner strength. We all do this, to some extent, unconsciously and under the press of exigency; but making what happens naturally into an intelligent program is a very human thing to do. Each individual can use imagination, knowledge of self, and personal difficulties to fashion personal techniques of willpower. And so, to get back to moralizing, this is how I want to leave you: with the challenge to come to *know* yourself, to become your own master in obedience to God who is the master of all, to become his partner in the task of becoming solid enough, single enough, centered enough to belong to the community of spirits that is the kingdom of God.

LIST OF WORKS CITED

Bloom, Anthony, *Beginning to Pray* (Paulist/Newman Press, 1970).

Epictetus, *Enchiridion*, tr. by Thomas W. Higginson (Bobbs-Merrill Co., 1955).

Hillesum, Etty, *Het Verstoorde Leven* (Haarlem: de Haan, 1981).

James, William, *Memories and Studies* (Greenwood Press, 1968).

———, *The Principles of Psychology*, 2 vols. (Dover Publications, 1950).

Johnson, Samuel, *The Works of Samuel Johnson, LL.D.* (Edinburgh: William Nimmo & Co., 1881).

Lawrence, Brother, *The Practice of the Presence of God* (Fleming H. Revell Co., 1956).

Leech, Kenneth, *True Prayer* (Harper & Row, 1980).

Malcolm, Norman, *Ludwig Wittgenstein: A Memoir* (Oxford University Press, 1958).

Muggeridge, Malcolm, *Something Beautiful for God* (Doubleday & Co., 1977).

Russell, Bertrand, *The Autobiography of Bertrand Russell 1872–1914* (Little, Brown & Co., 1951).

Steere, Douglas V., *On Being Present Where You Are* (Pendle Hill Pamphlet 151, 1967).

Thomas à Kempis, *The Imitation of Christ* (Moody Press, n.d.).

Ward, Benedicta, tr. and ed., *The Sayings of the Desert Fathers* (Cistercian Publications, 1975).

Wittgenstein, Ludwig, *Culture and Value*, ed. by G. H. von Wright and tr. by Peter Winch (University of Chicago Press, 1980).

www.ingramcontent.com/pod-product-compliance
Lightning Source LLC
Chambersburg PA
CBHW070929160426
43193CB00011B/1623